The Billionaire's Secret

How the World's Wealthiest
People Get Rich and Stay Rich
with Preferred Securities

Herbert Tabin

Contents

TOP SECRET

WHY YOU NEED TO READ THIS BOOK...

HAVE YOU EVER WONDERED HOW the ultra-wealthy get rich and then stay rich?

Do they know something you don't?

Amazingly, yes!

You see, while your cash is earning close to nothing in the bank, the ultra-rich are making 5, 10 and even 20% on that same amount of money. As you clutch a 2% certificate of deposit (CD) for dear life, the ultra-rich have investments in companies paying three, four and five times that and more.

And while your bonds are yielding 2 or 3% yearly, investors in some preferred shares are getting fixed payments of 2 or 3% a quarter!

My guess what you're thinking is, how can it be true?

How do they do it?

What's the secret?

To learn the answer...

follow my story...

and change your life forever.

Herb Tabin, December 2019

1

MEETING MARVIN

I'M GOING TO INTRODUCE you to Marvin. It was Marvin who shared the secret with me. So, I want to let you in on some of our conversations from the outset.

But first, I want you to know what Marvin rescued me from...

It wasn't until I moved into an upscale Florida neighborhood, filled with the ultra-rich and billionaires alike, that I was finally let in on "the secret". You see, I personally had the good fortune of being an investment banker in the 1990's. My business worked with dozens of dot com companies, going public, allowing me to retire young. Yes, I still did consulting work from time-to-time, but the bulk of my income came from dividends, interest and stock gains.

Like most of us, I did what many do with their retirement savings, I hired a few "money managers". It a was risky strategy, leaving my assets in the hands of self-proclaimed experts, hoping they performed.

Was it convenient?

Yes.

Was it frightening?

Very.

Leaving my assets in the hands of others meant that I had little control over how they invested. Soon thereafter I felt a constant feeling of unease as each major stock market fluctuation had me cringing causing me worry about being wiped out financially, in a huge crash. Sound familiar? As an investment banker I had seen many companies fail for a host of reasons which had taught me that "hope is not a strategy" and although I knew that to my core, sadly, I found myself relying on hope. I knew I had to make a change but to what and how?

As time went by, I continued this reckless behavior. Year-in-and-year-out I invested with these money managers hoping for the best. Some years were good, others not as good. Luckily, I avoided most big stock market downturns purely on instinct. How? Well, when I felt nervous about the market, I would call my money managers demanding they sell out and get into cash.

This strategy worked until one day it didn't. Finally, I missed the market signals and I got hit. In an instant my accounts were down huge. It was a stock market correction I did not see coming. Concerned, I called my investment managers looking for a strategy. Instead they told me they were sorry and over time we could work to get it back. While they were "sorry", I was more, sorry.

Frustrated, I went to my community gym to shake things off and then to our breakfast room. I sat with one of the men I had met casually over the years. His name was Marvin. I knew little about Marvin except that he was well off, I just did not know how well off at the time. Marvin saw me and noticed I was shaken. He asked what was bothering me. I told him I was "a little concerned" about the stock market. He replied, "ah don't worry about it". But I was worried. Very worried.

While I wanted to talk more, I had been taught as a child it was impolite to talk about personal money issues, so I rarely did so in social circles. What was most strange was the stock market that morning was not just down huge, but scary huge and there was Marvin eating his free, club bagel with the non-dairy cheese slices he had brought from home. Shockingly, Marvin didn't seem to have a care in the world. As a matter of fact, as I looked around, a few of the other men also sitting there were totally unalarmed.

Now let me preface it by saying these guys, at the country club, just weren't ordinary men. These were some of the most powerful men both now and in their day. One had run one of the largest credit card companies in the world. Another was a former Goldman Sachs division president. Each sat, occasionally glancing up from their coffee at a tv airing CNBC. While they sat peacefully, inside I was screaming in terror fearful about my holdings and these guys were just sitting there quietly planning their day.

Finally, I couldn't take it anymore and I leaned over to Marvin and whispered, "aren't you even a little worried about the market"?

Marvin looked up and replied: "No, why? Are you"? He then asked me a strange question. "Don't you own any preferred stock"? I was puzzled. I had been an investment banker. I passed my Series 7 and yet I had no idea what he was talking about.

I responded, "No, no I don't."

To which he replied, "Oh I guess you're not that wealthy after all kid." And within an instant, Marvin had sized me up. It was the tell of all tells. I now had no poker face. To Marvin my response simply said I was well off, but not that well off because obviously I did not know. Marvin then looked up at me grinning and said, "I've seen you around, you're a nice boy and today is a good day for you, today I'll let you in on - "the billionaire's secret."

For you to understand a bit more, I have to give you a visual. Marvin at the time was in his eighties. He's a thin tall man with genuine black hair from his genetic heritage, has a long black ponytail going down past his shoulders and to top it off he often wears a straw hat. Seeing him, you would think he would be the last guy you would take investment advice from, but then you would be wrong. Very wrong. Marvin is a self-made millionaire and possibly billionaire or close to it. Not the flashy well-known type billionaire. Marvin is more the kind billionaire who brings fake cheese from home to put on his free club bagel every day and shops at Costco.

Yet Marvin could buy and sell me who knows how many times over.

You see, Marvin is much more Warren Buffett than Donald Trump and – as an aside – he knows *both* of them.

2

MARVIN'S SECRET OF THE ULTRA RICH

T HAT'S RIGHT. I AM ACTUALLY introducing the secret you need this early in the book. Unusual. But I don't want to keep you hanging. I want to help you in the same way that Marvin helped me. He's an amazing man. He did it all. He hit the financial trifecta[1]. He had made money in his business, then in New York real estate and finally the stock market. One thing for sure about my man Marvin is, he is not about to lose his money.

Marvin began to explain how he got to where he was. He was smart and cautious and as a young man he formulated **a plan.**

He knew that *buying quality stocks in the strongest companies*; companies that were essential to either everyday life or the economy, you know… those "too big to fail" types, were the best way to mitigate risk. We called these companies "too necessary to fail."

Dividends were the second part of his formula. The companies had to be strong enough to pay substantial consistent dividends as well.

Last, he explained the importance of *compound interest* and *not selling*.

Marvin told me that, as a young man, his original goal was to own 1,000 shares of every major public utility in America. Electric, water, gas, you name

---

[1] 'Trifecta' – a run of three wins, especially in gambling

it. If the public needed its services and if it had a strong credit rating and paid a strong dividend… he bought!

He began by buying 100 shares of each security, whenever he had the money. Then, when the dividend was paid, he would reinvest those dividends, buying more shares. Over 50 years, Marvin has well exceeded his goal of 1,000 shares of each utility: as a matter of fact, through dividends, splits, compounding and decades of rising share prices, Marvin now owns more than 10,000 15,000 or 20,000 shares of each utility. Shares he was buying for $1 $2 or $5 now trade at $20, $50, $100, or $150 plus a piece, all financed by dividends, reinvestment, and price appreciation.

"So, was that the secret?" I asked

"No, it just illustrates the importance of dividends, reinvestment of dividends and time" he said. "The secret is that there is a way to earn even more".

More? I mean he was turning $100 and $500 investments into millions over time, how could there be any more?

Marvin went on to say that, while many utilities' common stock paid a good dividend rate, other strains of stock in the same public company paid an even higher rate and were actually safer to buy! *Why safer* I asked? Because these strains of stock sit higher on the company's capital structure near the bonds rather than on the bottom of the corporate structure like common stock. (Higher on the corporate structure near the bonds means you get paid first before the common holders). So, safer but pays more.

"But that's backwards from virtually all investments," I replied.

"In this case it's true," he said. "Best of all if this stock goes down a lot you can make much more money than the stated dividend rate boosting your overall yield. And even much more money at times if there is calamity you could seize upon. In bad markets," he said, "you could be earning 10, 20 or 30% a year on the investment for the rest of its life or until it's matured or called." My mouth was agape. Could it even be possible to make 30% a year from a safe utility stock… and for life at that?

Marvin put down his coffee and said, "Today I am going to teach you the secrets of **preferred stock**."

"So *that's* the billionaires secret? Preferred stock?"

"Yes," Marvin said, "and if you follow my rules you will watch your money grow exponentially while everyone else just treads water." Then he added, "let's hope the stock market goes down a lot today, because then we can make even more money!"

From that day on I never worried about the stock market going down again. I learned that the worst days in the stock market are often the best days when you are a preferred stock investor.

Marvin then started talking to me about The **Rule of 72** and why it bears repeating. "It's a rule," he said, "that must be respected and followed." He went on to explain: "To understand how you can use your preferred stock to make money with the market up or down, we need to understand a bit about **how much you need to make yearly** in order **to grow your net worth.**" Cue next chapter!

3

THE RULE OF 72

I'M GUESSING YOU HAVE heard of it before. If not, "The Rule of 72" is a simple way of showing how long an investment will take to double, given a fixed annual rate of interest.

The formula for the rule is simple. By just dividing 72 by the annual rate of return, you can get an estimate of how many years it will take for your original investment to duplicate itself.

For example, $1 invested at 10% would take approximately 7.2 years to turn into $2. (72 divided by 10 = 7.2 years). In actuality, a 10% investment will take 7.3 years to double but that math gets prickly so for ease let's stick with the Rule of 72 formula; just dividing 72 by the annual rate of return, as an estimate.

But what if you wanted to double your money twice in one decade instead?

Do the math: 72 divided by 15 = 4.96.

So, you would need to get a 15% return which would double your investment approximately every 5 years[2].

Marvin said, "you see, you have to shoot for 10% a year on your

---

[2] If you do not feel like doing the rule of 72 calculation yourself, just go to this free website that will do the figuring out for you:
http://www.moneychimp.com/features/rule72.htm

investments but really you're shooting for 15%... so you can double your money twice next decade."

I replied, "that seems a bit lofty Marvin. How are we going to do that, and won't it take a lot of risk?"

"Patience! We're getting there!" he said. "Just remember, most preferred shares have paid 6% dividends historically which gets us almost halfway to 10% already".

This *napkinfinance.com* graphic shows the time it will take to double your money according to the Rule of 72.

Figure 1

Certificates of Deposits and Savings Accounts

I understood what Marvin was saying. We have to get, minimally, **10% a year to double our money**. So, I asked him, "why not buy some bank certificates of deposit [CD's] instead and take all the risk away? I mean, you can buy up to $250,000 per institution and have zero risk. Right?"

Marvin looked at me, half-perturbed, half-amused, and said, "Are you listening to me? Unless the bank is giving you 7% on a CD, or higher, absolutely not! Today's CD's pay 2% or so and if we look again at the Rule of 72, we can see exactly why CD investments and low rates do not perform for you".

Then he stopped me dead cold. "Did you ever hear Robert G. Allen's expression – **'How many millionaires do you know who have become wealthy by investing in savings accounts? I rest my case.'?**"

"No."

"Well don't forget it! No one gets rich investing in basic savings accounts. No one". He continued, "sure savings accounts are virtually a sure bet, but the gains will be small given the low risk. People have to stop looking at CD's as a good low risk investment. They are not! CD's do have their place – to put money into *for the interim* – but, as a long-term investment idea, they are terrible. The risk you take buying a 1-2% CD is huge."

Let's have a look at why, by going back right now to the **Rule of 72**.

Certificates of Deposit and the Rule of 72

Explaining why CD's weren't a good choice lit Marvin up. I loved seeing the passion that his experience and knowledge gave him! He began, "Let's look at the facts using the Rule of 72. Suppose that the bank is offering a CD rate of 2% on your money: it's FDIC-insured, and you know (barring great calamity) you are getting your money back. Sounds good, right? But now, apply the Rule of 72..."

His eyes narrowed. "How long it will take you to double your money? Are you ready? The answer is shocking! 36 years. That's right... 36 years! So, if you were a 25-year-old with $100,000 to invest, wanting the safest return possible – CD's or treasury notes paying 2% – you would not see your money double until you were 61 years old!

"So, let's look at that 25-year-old with CD's 36 years later. The crucial question involves a comparison: now that, 36 years after his investment, he has doubled his money, what is that amount worth in real terms?" To help illustrate this question, Marvin asked me another more personal question. "How much did your parents buy their first house for, and when?"

I replied "$27,000 in 1969".

"Well imagine they had the money and instead of buying a home they bought a 2% CD. Let's look 36 years later from 1969 to 2005. How much do you think your parent's home was worth in 2005, 36 years later?"

"They sold their home for **$400,000** around that time", I answered.

"Exactly!" Marvin replied. "Their home increased in value X times, now look at the CD, $27,000 at 2% and 36 years later it's worth only **$54,000**.

"Was that a good investment"?

"No," I answered, struck by the difference between the two outcomes.

UNDERSTANDING THE
RULE OF 72

The Rule of 72 is an easy compound interest calculation to estimate how long it will take to double your money.

72 ÷ Interest rate = Years to double money

Using the rates shown, here is about how long it would take to double an initial investment.

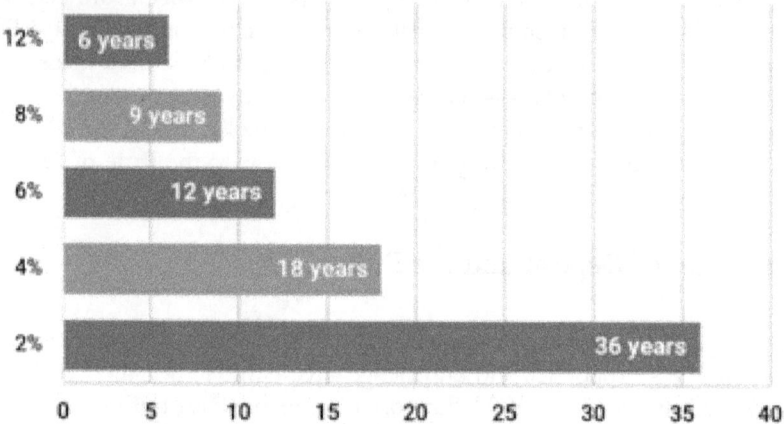

12%	6 years
8%	9 years
6%	12 years
4%	18 years
2%	36 years

0   5   10   15   20   25   30   35   40

SOURCE: St. Louis Fed Econ Lowdown, "It's Your Paycheck."

FEDERAL RESERVE BANK of ST. LOUIS

Figure 2

Marvin said, "Look… the reality is that 2% CD's are a great deal for the bank, who use it to lend at higher rates, but *for you*, whether you're 25, 61 or any other age… it's a *terrible* deal. At 2% interest you are going backwards, losing money every year due mainly to inflation. The only investment worse than that is a passbook savings account or interest-bearing checking account which would take 72 years to double.

"As preferred stock investors," yep, Marvin was including me in his world already, "remember our desire is to return *at minimum* 10% per year: so that in 7.3 years, we double our money. Again, if we return 15%, we double our money in fewer than 5 years or twice in a decade."

"Marvin, I am sold on the fact that CD's are not a good investment long term, but I don't want to take a lot of risk."

Marvin replied, "I am not asking you take great risks. Let me explain why the stockbrokers have tricked you into thinking you need to take great risks to get these returns. Also, I'll explain why we cannot lose our money because of the reality of loss… and then we can get back to the good stuff: the secret!" Secrets, tricks, realities; it was all good stuff to me! Marvin Magic.

Risk and Stockbroker Trickery

"As a man investing for more than 60 years I have been pitched over and over by money managers large and small who all insist that, 'to make money you need to take risk.' I say bullshit!

"Let me clear this up. The notion that "risk" itself makes you money is fake. False nonsense. It's just a stockbroker's sales line used to separate you from your money. Sounds convincing right? Kinda logical? 'You got to risk money to make money.'

"Amazingly, this sales pitch works.

"But, **in reality**, it's nothing more than a devious plan to protect the money manager's ass. You see, later, when those same money managers *do* lose you money, they then circle back blaming that same "risk" which you seemed so sold on in the first place. They can say they told you so. To them it's "too bad, so sad" and onto the next risk taker. Meanwhile, your savings are gone, and you have little recourse.

"In the future when you hear "**risk**," replace it with "**danger**." Do not take it lightly! It took you a long time to accumulate the money you have, and you don't want to give it away. On Wall Street it's easier to lose money than it is to make it. Always keep in mind the words of Mark J. Grant - the preferred stock guru – **"Risk is a monster and we do not like monsters."**

"That's not to say there isn't risk in preferred stock or any other investment. The key here is to eliminate those investments based on risk and replace them with investments that carry a lesser degree of risk, a risk that can be identified and mitigated. Once we substantially reduce our risk, we can put a plan in place.

"We must preserve our capital because of what it takes to make it back."

Preservation of Capital

Marvin told me that Warren Buffett loves to say:

The first rule of investment is do not lose money. And the second rule of investment is don't forget the first rule. And that's all the rules there are.

Marvin himself loves to say…

It is much easier to keep your hard-earned money than make more money.

True, this seems a little counter-intuitive in a book about investment. But I haven't lost the plot! Marvin's lesson here really is to **preserve your capital**. Losses are much, much, harder to recover from than most people think, hence the expression Marvin saw on my face that morning over breakfast as I worried about the markets crashing! Stockbrokers discount the risks. I'm not sure that most investors understand what it takes to recover from a stock loss in price.

How big is the problem?

Well, Marvin explained it to me like this…

"Do you know how hard it is to recover from a stock that declines in price?"

I said "no".

He continued, "if your stock goes down and you have a 35% loss from your purchase price, in order for you to get even that stock has to recover a 54% gain in share price. It magnifies with a bigger loss: a 50% loss requires a 100% gain and a 60% loss requires a 150% gain."

Marvin knows. I was shocked. Take a look how difficult it is to recover using the percentage recovery formula below. Here are the mathematics involved when a stock declines:

Percentage Recovery Formula

The mathematical formula for percentage loss to getting back to even is:

$$y = x/(1-x)$$

where 'y' is the percentage gain required to break even and 'x' is the percentage lost.

Which means that:

Recovering from a 5% loss requires a 5.2% gain
Recovering from a 10% loss requires a 11% gain
Recovering from a 15% loss requires a 18% gain
Recovering from a 20% loss requires a 25% gain

Recovering from a 25% loss requires a 33% gain
Recovering from a 30% loss requires a 43% gain
Recovering from a 35% loss requires a 54% gain
Recovering from a 40% loss requires a 67% gain
Recovering from a 45% loss requires an 82% gain
Recovering from a 50% loss requires a 100% gain
Recovering from a 60% loss requires a 150% gain

This percentage recovery formula is a real eye-opener, as most people do not realize what it genuinely takes to recover from a loss. Now that you have the knowledge –

Hold onto your money as if they are not going to make
any more!
– Gary Coleman

Now that we know to go for a **10%** return, **limit** our risk, and **preserve** our capital… it's time to get back to **preferred stock!**

4

PREFERRED STOCK

PREFERRED STOCK IS ONE OF the world's greatest and most misunderstood investments. It has all the elements of success for both the issuer and the investor and those elements, magically, are unique to just **preferred shares** and their kissing cousin **exchange traded debt**[3].

What is Preferred Stock?

To make things simple, think of preferred stock as if a common stock and a bond married and had a baby. Knowing the parents, what could we assume about the baby?

Well, we would assume that the baby, as the product of *both* parents, has the traits of both: part-stock and part-bond.

In a nutshell that's exactly what a preferred stock is; a security that **trades like a stock but acts like a bond**.

Let's see at *what* makes it trade like a stock and then what makes it act like a bond.

---

[3] see chapter 5

Stock DNA

Just like its common stock parent, preferred stock trades on a listed exchange, like the *New York Stock Exchange*. It has a stock symbol and looks like a common stock. Preferred stock is also bought and sold exactly the same way you would buy and sell common stock. Simple enough.

Bond DNA

Just like its bond parent, preferred stock pays a yearly fixed dividend such as 5%, 6% or 7% or more, when it is sold by **the issuer**, the preferred stock's underlying company. Dividends are paid quarterly or semi-annually. (See the table on the next page for how much each dividend is per quarter or year based on its dividend rate).

Preferred stock, when issued, is often sold in denominations of $25, $50, $100 and even $1,000 per share. This is known as the "face value" or "par value" and is the same amount used later when shares can be bought back, or 'redeemed' or '**called**' (they are 'called back' to the issuer at maturity).

In other words, for the issuer to buy back the preferred shares, they *have* to pay you the price of what the shares were originally issued at or sold for *at par*. So, if you bought preferred shares at $25 per share, when those shares are **called** or redeemed, the price the issuer will pay you is the original $25 per share you bought them at.

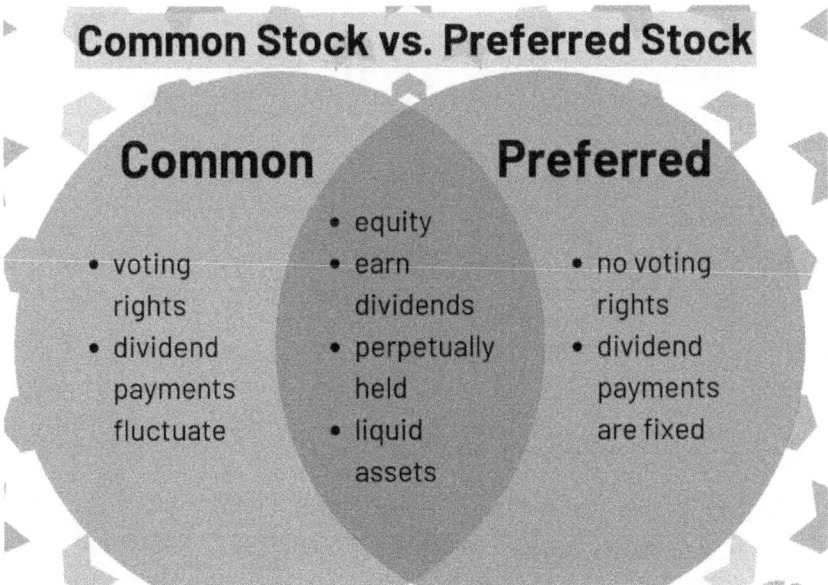

Common Stock vs. Preferred Stock

Common

- voting rights
- dividend payments fluctuate

- equity
- earn dividends
- perpetually held
- liquid assets

Preferred

- no voting rights
- dividend payments are fixed

Figure 3

Dividend Chart

Dividend Rate	Dividend Per Quarter	Dividend Per Year
3%	**$0.1875**	**$0.75**
3.125%	$0.1953	$0.78125
3.25%	$0.203125	$0.8125
3.5%	$0.12875	$0.875
3.625%	$0.2265	$0.90625
3.75%	$0.2343	$0.9375
3.875%	$0.2421	$0.96.875
4%	**$0.25**	**$1.00**
4.125%	$0.257	$1.03125
4.25%	$0.2656	$1.0625
4.5%	$0.28125	$1.125
4.625%	$0.2890	$1.15625
4.75%	$0.296875	$1.1875
4.875%	$0.3046875	$1.21875
5%	**$0.3125**	**$1.25**
5.125%	$0.3203	$1.28125
5.25%	$0.3281	$1.3125
5.5%	$0.34375	$1.375
5.625%	$0.3515	$1.40625
5.75%	$0.3593	$1.4375
5.875%	$0.3671	$1.46875
6%	**$0.375**	**$1.50**
6.125%	$0.3828	$1.53125
6.25%	$0.3906	$1.5625
6.5%	$0.40625	$1.625
6.625%	$0.4140	$1.65625
6.75%	$0.4218	$1.6875
6.875%	$0.4296	$1.71875
7%	**$0.4375**	**$1.75**
7.125%	$0.44531	$1.78125
7.25%	$0.4531	$1.8125
7.5%	$0.46875	$1.875
7.625%	$0.4765	$1.90625
7.75%	$0.4843	$1.9375
7.875%	$0.4921	$1.96875
8%	**$0.50**	**$2.00**
8.125%	$0.5078	$2.03125
8.25%	$0.5156	$2.0625
8.5%	$0.53125	$2.125
8.625%	$0.539	$2.15625
8.75%	$0.5468	$2.1875
8.875%	$0.5546	$2.21875
9%	**$0.5625**	**$2.25**
9.125%	$0.5703	$2.28125

$

WHY PREFERRED STOCK PAYS MORE

AFTER A QUICK EXPLANATION I understood what Marvin was imparting to me about what a preferred stock was, but that only raised more questions. Marvin had said the preferred shares paid high dividends and were safer. All I thought was, *how could that be?*

Marvin boiled it down to a couple of things, starting with the corporate structure.

What is a Company's Capital Structure?

"It all boils down to capital structure", Marvin said. "As an investor, you want to be **as high on that structure as you can be**."

As an investment banker, I was well aware of what Marvin was referring to: a company's **capital structure** reflects all of its equity and debt obligations. Its capital structure shows the types of obligations as a level in a stack. Think of a stack of coins. There are those coins that are on the bottom and those that are on the top. The coins at the top of the pile depend on the

'Think of a stack of coins.'

coins below them, propping them up, but are not necessarily of a greater value. But in a company's capital structure, this stack is **ranked by risk** and **the priority each stacked coin** has in a liquidation event, such as bankruptcy.

For large corporations, the stack typically consists of:

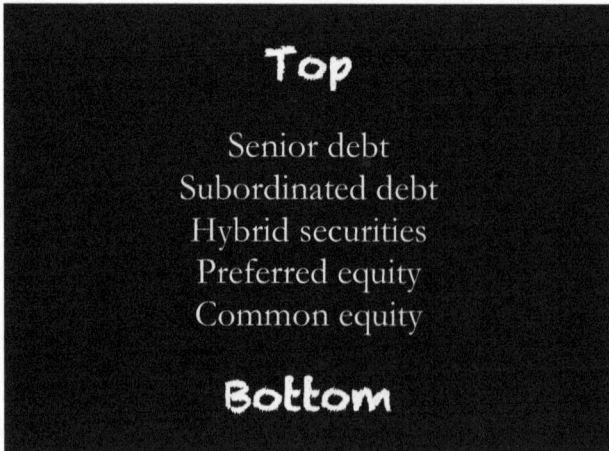

The Components

Sounds confusing but it isn't. Let's start at the top, with the senior debt.

Senior Debt

This is the highest loan class with the highest priority on the repayment list if a company goes bankrupt.

What does that mean?

It means that if you're a holder of the senior debt and the company goes bad then you have first dibs on the company's assets over all other classes of debt and equity. You are in the best spot to get money back because, in the event of liquidation, senior creditors are paid in full *first*, before lenders holding lesser debt, like subordinated notes, are paid.

Because it is the lowest risk on the capital structure being at the top of the stack, senior lenders can and do loan money at lower rates relative to lower tiers.

Makes sense! Most security, lowest risk, lowest loan rates.

Subordinated Debt

This is the next class down of loans, ranked below senior debt with regard to claims on assets. Being lower on the capital structure the loan becomes more risky than senior borrowings. As such it also comes with higher returns, usually in the form of higher interest payments.

Preferred Equity

Moving down the list we hit preferred shares, a class of financing representing ownership interest in a company that has both debt and equity characteristics in the form of fixed dividends (debt) and future earnings potential (equity). As such, it gives the holder both upside and downside exposure.

Preferred claims on the company's assets come *behind* those of debt holders (senior and subordinated) but *ahead* of common stockholders. Most importantly, preferred equity obligates management to pay its holders a predetermined dividend before paying out dividends to common shareholders. On the downside, preferred equity typically comes without voting rights.

Common Equity

Common equity is the lowest section of the capital structure and therefore represents ownership in a business *after* all other obligations have been paid down. As such it has the highest risk and the highest potential returns of any tier in the capital structure.

Simple Capital Structure Illustration

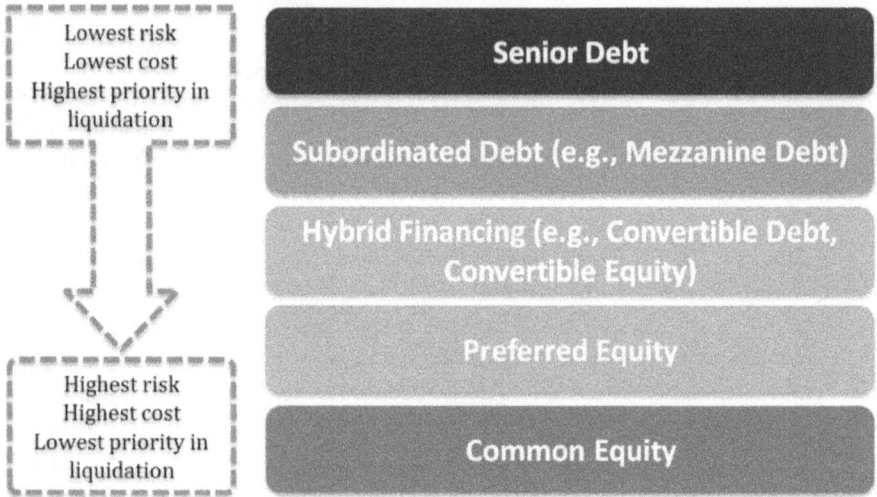

```
Lowest risk                   Senior Debt
Lowest cost
Highest priority in    Subordinated Debt (e.g., Mezzanine Debt)
liquidation
                       Hybrid Financing (e.g., Convertible Debt,
                                  Convertible Equity)

                                 Preferred Equity
Highest risk
Highest cost
Lowest priority in              Common Equity
liquidation
```

Figure 4 courtesy Axial.net

The Capital Structure's Purpose

The capital structure is basically an overview of all the claims on the business. **Debt holders** hold claims of cash owed to them (i.e., the principal) and their interest payments. **Equity owners** hold claims in the form of access to a percentage of that company's future profit.

The capital structure determines how risky it is to invest in a company, and how expensive financing should be. All else being equal, getting additional capital for a business with a debt-heavy capital structure is more expensive than getting that same funding for a business with an equity-heavy capital structure. More debt – higher borrowing costs.

How Capital Structure Drives Demand for Preferred Shares

To understand what drives investors to own preferred stock, answer this question:

As an investor, do you want to be paid sooner or later if an issuer is having financial problems and needs to liquidate?

The obvious answer is **sooner**.
The next question becomes,

How do you get to a better place in the line?

Answer: be as **close to the top** of a company's capital structure as possible.

Let's look at that basic public company corporate structure again.

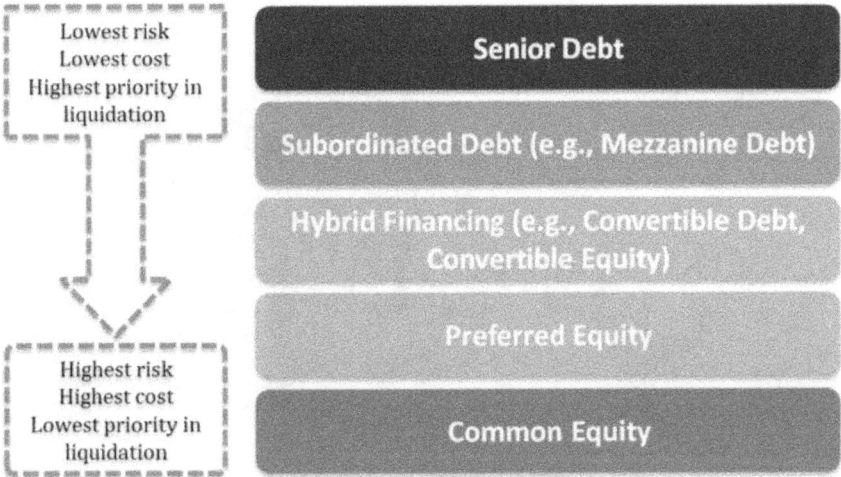

Lowest risk Lowest cost Highest priority in liquidation	**Senior Debt**
	Subordinated Debt (e.g., Mezzanine Debt)
	Hybrid Financing (e.g., Convertible Debt, Convertible Equity)
	Preferred Equity
Highest risk Highest cost Lowest priority in liquidation	**Common Equity**

Who will get paid first if the company has to liquidate?

Senior debt gets paid first.
Second the subordinated debt.
Then hybrid.
Then preferred stock and lastly…
Common stock.

What shocks me every time I show people the corporate structure is how most people are amazed that when they buy common stock they are buying on the absolute bottom. Strangely, most just don't even realize what they have been buying for decades. Think about it. If a company you held shares in was to liquidate or go into bankruptcy, it's the common shareholders who are dead last to get paid, and only then if anything at all is left.

Aside from being the first in the queue for payment, one other advantage of sitting **high up** on the capital structure is that there is **less volatility** up there. There is less volatility because there is more security. Imagine being chased by a tiger: the higher up the tree you can climb and sit and wait, the more secure you are. Security equals protection. Being higher on the capital structure provides more security, as with *secured* bonds. At the same time, it follows that the bottom of the capital structure (like common stock) is the least secure place to be and has the most volatility. Closer to that tiger!

So as a basic rule of investing *from a safety perspective*, you want to invest closer to the top of a company's capital structure because if that issuer declares bankruptcy, the creditors at the top of the structure will get paid first and the equity holders at the bottom will get paid last.

So, What's the Trade-Off?

Remember, no common stockholders can be paid one penny in dividends until all the preferred holders have been fully paid. Hence, their preference.

The catch? To be paid first and be "preferred" holders typically do not have voting rights like holders of common stock. While in the abstract this is disheartening, the reality is that unless you hold millions of shares in a public company, your vote has absolutely no weight in any decision-making anyway.

Credit Rating

As we saw above with the simple public company capital structure, preferred stock sits higher than common stock but below bonds. As a result, a company's preferred stock credit rating is generally lower than that of its bonds, but higher than that of common stock.

This is important.

All this occurs because of who is in line to be paid. Because a lower placement in the capital structure is below the bonds, **risk increases** causing preferred shares to pay higher dividend rates.

"Baby Bonds" or
"Kissing Cousins"

BEFORE WE CONTINUE, WE must discuss preferred stock's 'kissing cousin' **Exchange Traded Debt Security**. **ETDS** (also known as 'baby bonds') and **preferred stock** are often confused.

So, What's the Difference between Them?

Exchange Traded Debt Securities are notes and bonds that are *traded on the stock exchange* with a stock symbol, just like preferred shares, *instead of on the bond markets*. They carry maturities of 30 years or more (although some are just 5-10 years).

Most exchange traded debt issues are 'junior' to the company's secured debt and 'senior' to preferred and common shares.

Although similar to preferred shares, ETDS pay quarterly interest payments (not dividends), have a $25 par value, and are callable after 5 years.

Why interest?

Due to the fact that ETDS are listed on the issuers books as *debt* rather than *equity* they pay out interest rather than dividends. As opposed to preferred shares which pay dividends out of company cash flow.

Brokerages mistake these securities as preferred stock all the time, but ETDS are actually a superior security to preferred stocks and offer lower risk. As a form of bond, ETDS have a slightly stronger credit rating than preferred stock as they also have a higher ranking in the issuer's capital structure. Higher ranking means more likely to be paid on default. Bondholders therefore sit higher than preferred shareholders, making them safer in the event of company liquidation.

(Throughout, this book wide will refer to the two synonymously for simplicity.)

6

OLDER THAN MARVIN

I OFTEN JOKE WITH Marvin who is now in his nineties that the reason he knows so much about preferred shares is because he was around at their beginning. The reality is, of course, that – although not quite 'as old as the hills' – preferred shares *are* much older than *Marvin*! And as you'll see, these shares have come a long way from their roots.

Years ago, preferred stock was relegated to a small corner of Wall Street reserved for companies such as railroads and public utilities. In fact, the history of preferred stock goes back over a hundred and fifty years and financed a lot of the infrastructure we still use today. For example, you might even recall the name *Tennessee Valley Authority* or the *TVA* from history classes in elementary school.

The TVA, if you remember, was a federally owned corporation started during the Great Depression that was two-fold by design. The project was intended to create thousands of new jobs in one of the poorest regions in the country, the Tennessee Valley and its surrounding areas. Secondly the TVA was to bring hydroelectric power to those people.

It was a private/public partnership, project-financed in part by the government and in part by the public. The financing of the project was arranged in the year 1929 and **part of it was set up using preferred stock**. At the time, the maturity date on the preferred stock (or the termination date or due date on which the TVA preferred shares mature and must be bought back) was set at 100 years later: 2029.

Well, not only has TVA preferred stock financed the Tennessee Valley Authority, but it is still thriving and one of the largest power utilities in the USA. More remarkable still: Tennessee Valley Authority preferred shares *still* trade on the stock market to this day!

Known by traders nowadays as "Uncle Dam" (a take-off of Uncle Sam because of its close association with the United States government), the TVA is one of the longest paying dividend preferred stocks in existence with a credit rating almost equal to the United States government itself and a pay out of 3-4%.

Had You Only Known!

Decades ago, average CD yields exceeded 10%. You won't find a return anywhere close to that today. As you may recall, starting in early 2000, the economy started to slow. To pick up speed, the Federal Reserve lowered interest rates. Back then the average yield on 1-year CDs dipped below 2% in 2002.

In 2009, after the financial crisis, the average 12-month CD paid just 1.16%. Average rates on 5-year CDs were slightly higher (2.21%). Other rates fell, as the central bank brought its key interest rate down to its lowest point possible.

The Federal Reserve's efforts to stimulate the economy following the Great Recession left many banks so flush with cash that they held on to their extra funds, meaning that they didn't have to boost CD rates to obtain money for lending. This resulted in CD rates reaching historic lows.

In 2013, average yields on 1-year and 5-year CDs were 0.24% and 0.8% respectively.

A decade after the Great Recession, CDs have finally budged. In fact, the average 1-year CD pays 1.85%, according to *Bankrate*'s most recent national survey of banks and thrifts.

One thing to think about is that over the last two decades as interest rates sunk to near zero, had you owned either of the TVA preferred shares (TVC or TVE) rather than any bank CD, money market accounts, or savings account you would have been earning 3-4% on your money instead. Simply investing in 'Uncle Dam' preferred shares with its credit rating that's equal to the USA government meant that, during that time, you got as much as three to four times the CD rate on your money – with a security virtually safe as the treasury's. Had you only known!

Now I know what many of you are thinking. That you are going to run out right now and buy some of those Uncle Dams and double the CD or treasury percentage rate that you're getting right now. While there's nothing wrong with the rate, return and safety of Uncle Dams, there are many similar investments that pay **even higher rates**: up to 9% plus.

We will get to those in a moment. The key point is that when interest rates are low, preferred stock dividends are much higher than bank CDs and treasury or corporate bonds.

The Modern Day '$25 Par Preferred' Is Invented

As for preferred shares, things have changed a lot since the early days of the TVA. Back then, there were just 20-100 preferred stock issues trading and, while the number of issues grew minimally for years, that all changed when *Texaco, Inc.* – the largest of the oil companies – altered the game forever in the 1990's, by shifting the preferred stock market from *institutional* investors to *retail* investors.

Texaco's Preferred Stock Shift

Institutional Investors ⟶ **Retail Investors**

THE PUBLIC!

Prior to its introduction in 1993, Texaco's new **$25 par preferred security** set the stage for the future of all preferred stocks. Not only was this share cheaper than those of the past which were typically set at $1,000 or $100 par, it was also structured more **like a bond** and listed on the NYSE; a place where retail investors were already familiar with buying and selling stocks.

Texaco's Preferred Stock Shift (2)

$1000/$100 ⟶ **$25**

MORE ACCESSIBLE!

Texaco's development of this new **$25 par, retail-oriented, preferred securities market** (bit of a mouthful that!) tapped a new larger investor base for issuers: the public!

From a capital-raising perspective, the issuer had the new benefit of being able to choose the market with the best demand and pricing dynamics. Texaco specifically set security at $25 par so that retail investors could buy small lots of the shares. This differed from the corporate bond market which traded, **Over-The-Counter** bonds in large lot sizes, making it less accessible to retail investors.

Today there are over 1,000 different preferred issues trading; ranging from utilities to real estate investment trusts, conglomerates and more with those that offer $25 par preferred securities still dominating the market.

How Are They Used?

Today preferred shares are used regularly to finance all types of businesses. Let's take a look at the industries financed by preferred shares.

Preferred Shares, by Industry

- Automotive
- Banking and Savings
- Business Services and Equipment
- Closed End Funds
- Consumer Goods
- Drugs and Pharmaceutical
- Energy
- Financial
- Industrial
- Insurance
- Metals and Mining
- Oil and Gas
- Real Estate
- REITS
- Shipping
- Technology
- Transportation
- Utilities

Preferred shares and exchange traded debt are issued by most major corporations in America today. When you're buying preferred shares, they're mostly from names you will know.

Here are a few examples by industry

Marquee Names of Companies Offering Preferred Shares or Exchange Traded Debt, by Industry

- Automotive - Ford
- Banking and Savings – Bank of America, Wells Fargo, Citigroup
- Business Services and Equipment – Pitney Bowes
- Closed End Funds – Legg Mason
- Consumer Goods – Stanley Black and Decker, Brunswick
- Drugs and Pharmaceutical – Becton Dickinson
- Energy – NuStar, DCP
- Financial - Goldman Sachs, JP Morgan
- Industrial – Navistar, International Paper
- Insurance – AIG, Allstate, Met Life
- Metals and Mining – Helca Mining
- Oil and Gas - DynaGas
- Real Estate – Public Storage
- REITS – Vornado, Simon
- Shipping – Seaspan
- Technology – EBAY, AT&T
- Transportation - Costamare
- Utilities – Southern Company, Duke Energy, Next Era

Pitfalls of New Preferred Shares

One thing to emphasize before moving on is that – just because a security is a "preferred" share does not make it "safe". Today many low demand new issues come to market offering high dividends as incentive to raise money. Beware! More choice *seems* better but, as preferred stocks have moved away from traditional issuers like utilities and railroads, the risks have grown exponentially.

The **preferred stocks that we are talking about** are *meant to be a safe investment*. Always keep that in mind and do not allow yourself to be lured by high yield, lower quality companies. **We only want to buy quality issuers.** This is *our* money we are investing.

In the next few chapters you'll be shown how to identify and separate the strong candidates for investment from the weak ones.

7

WHY PREFERRED STOCK?

W HEN MARVIN AND I first started discussing preferred stock the first question I asked him was "so why do investors buy preferred stock"?

Marvin replied "because it pays the most! It pays more in dividends than just about everything and preferred stock has been one of the highest yielding sectors in the fixed income market period!"

It's true more often than not, dividends from preferred shares pay much higher yields than common stock and even investment-grade corporate bonds. As a general rule of thumb, preferred stock typically pays triple, yes triple, the rate you can earn off a bank CD.

"Don't wait until everything is just right. It will never be perfect. There will always be challenges, obstacles and less than perfect conditions. So, what. Get started now. With each step you take, you will grow stronger and stronger, more and more skilled, more and more self-confident and more and more successful."
—Mark Victor Hansen

What Preferred Stock Offers over Other Investments

Let's talk about what other things make preferred shares… well… *preferred!*

i.e.

- Higher Yield
- Income Frequency
- Quality
- Lower Volatility
- Diversification
- Liquidity
- Cumulative Dividends
- Trading Flexibility
- Investment Grade Securities
- Seniority

Higher Yield[4]

Preferred securities are one of the highest yielding sectors of the **fixed income market**. Typically, **investment grade** preferred shares pay dividend rates between 5 and 9% a year. Rarely do preferred shares yield over 10% or under 3%. Preferred shares usually trade at an attractive rate, or **spread[5]**, over the same issuer's senior debt.

In other words, while a company's bonds may pay 4% interest, their preferred shares may pay 6% in dividends.

As such, when the company's debt rating is stable or improving, investment in a junior subordinated instrument – like preferred securities – creates the potential for a higher yield and return than debt issued higher in the company's capital structure. This is called **investing down the capital structure**.

Income Frequency

Preferred $25 par securities pay dividends quarterly, like common stock.

---

[4] For the definition of 'yield', see next chapter.
[5] There are several definitions of the term 'spread' within the investment context, but they all basically refer to the difference between two prices or yields.

Preferred $50, $100, $1,000 par securities typically pay semi-annual dividends, like corporate bonds. With preferred shares, unlike common shares, you know the dividend rate you are going to receive for the life of the security and the exact dates on which you will get those payments. This information is found within the company's prospectus or offering documents.

Quality

Most preferred securities are issued by well-known and well-researched companies that are rated 'investment grade'.

Lower Volatility

Because preferred stocks have a fixed dividend rate, they do not fluctuate the way common stocks do. When the market changes, they can potentially reduce the overall volatility of an equity or high yield portfolio. Less speculation often translates to less market price volatility compared to common stocks. Keep in mind, however, that preferred stocks will always be more volatile than traditional fixed income and can carry **more risk** when financial sectors are under pressure.

Diversification

Preferred shares offer diversification for fixed income investors.

Liquidity

Most preferred securities markets are thought of as "liquid," whereby most securities can be sold *immediately* with others being sold within a few hours. Unlike CDs or other investments, **preferred securities are traded on a stock exchange**. With preferred stock, you can **track** and **trade** shares whenever the markets are open.

Cumulative Dividends

Unlike common stock dividends, many preferred dividends are what's called **cumulative**, meaning that *if an issuer misses* a dividend payment (or several dividend payments) that issuer still *owes* you the money for those missed dividend payments.

They accumulate.

So, in the future if they are able to pay again, they must pay the shareholder all dividends missed and owed. Further, no future common stock dividend payments can be made to any common shareholder until all the preferred shareholders are paid first.

Trading Flexibility

With preferred stock you can enter **market limit offers** to buy or sell preferred shares or use **stop-loss orders** to manage risk.

Investment Grade Securities

The majority of preferred securities issued are well-known, solid, well-researched companies with investment grade-rated senior debt. Historically, most of the additional return generated by preferred securities is attributable to its *call option* premium and *junior subordination*.

Seniority

Preferred shares are senior to common stock, meaning that the issuing company will make dividend payments on preferred stock *before* making payments on common stock. However, preferred stock generally has a lower credit rating than bonds issued by the same company as they sit lower in the capital structure of the issuer.

So, now we know what it is that makes preferred shares desirable, we need to understand **yield** more fully…

8

YIELD

B EFORE WE GO ANY further into Marvin's secret, I just want to make sure everyone understands what yield is; as yield is a large part of preferred investing and preferred securities.

What is Yield?

Yield is **earnings realized on an investment over a time**, shown as **a percentage** – *based on* the invested amount and its current market value, or the face value of the security. It includes the dividends, or interest, earned or received from holding that security.

Types and Examples of Yields

Current Yield - CY
This is calculated by dividing the annual coupon payment (amount paid by interest or dividend for the year) by the current market price of the security.

Let's use this example of a preferred share with an annual coupon payment of $1.50 per year trading at $25. For this preferred share the current yield would be 6% or $1.50 divided by $25 = 6%. Now, *what if the coupon* *payment is the same $1.50 per year but the preferred share is trading higher at $27?* The current yield would drop to be 5.55% or $1.50 divided by $27 = 5.55%.

When the share price goes up the current yield goes down.

Conversely, *what if the coupon payment is $1.50 per year and the preferred share is now trading down at $22?* The current yield would be 6.8% or $1.50 divided by $22 = 6.8%. So, when the share price goes down the current yield goes up.

That means to get a greater current yield, buy shares lower.

Yield-To-Maturity - YTM

This is the yield that results if the preferred share is held to final maturity and dividends are reinvested at the yield-to-maturity rate, taking into account the income earned and any capital gain or loss that will be made.

For example, if an investor has to consider redemption or selling back their shares at a lower price for a preferred share bought at a premium (meaning they paid more than par) and held to maturity, the holder will only receive the par at maturity.

Yield-To-Call - YTC

This is the yield if a security is held until the first call date, assuming all dividends are reinvested at the call rate and taking into account any income and any capital gains or losses.

Yield-To-Worst -YTW

Generally, if a preferred share is trading above par, the yield to call will be lower as the preferred share is likely to be called. However, if the preferred share is trading *at* or *below par*, the yield to maturity will be higher and so is less likely to be called.

The Difference Between Dividends and Interest

It sounds silly but most people confuse interest and dividends. It's not a terrible mistake but can be important regarding taxes. The difference is easy to remember though: **stocks** pay **dividends** and **bonds** pay **interest**.

Bond Interest

Bonds pay interest. When you buy a bond, you are essentially lending money to a company for a period of time. In exchange for your lending money, the bond company pays you interest on that money on a schedule up until the date the company pays you back your principal.

As such your loan and all loans by others appear on the books of the issuing bond company as debt, as the company is in debt or "indebted" to you and all the others who have lent it money. This results in the borrowing company being allowed to deduct (subtract) that interest it pays you off of their taxes as a business expense. Conversely you as the bondholder who receives the interest will be taxed on that interest.

Common Stock Dividends

When you buy common stock, there are no promises of a return or any obligation to pay you any type of return. As a common stockholder you are what's called an **equity holder**, meaning, you are technically one of the company's owners by owning shares as a shareholder. This is called having an **equity position**.

Now, if the company becomes profitable, the company can choose to pay out a portion of those profits to you. That bit of profit paid out to you is called a **dividend**. A dividend is simply a payout of a portion of the profits, known as a distribution of profits to all the owners. These profits, which are distributed, are not taxed before you receive them. These dividends or profits are also known as **dividend income**. As an owner/shareholder who receives this non-taxed dividend income, you are then responsible to pay the taxes on your profits.

What about Preferred Stock?

When you buy preferred stock, you're buying shares of a stock which makes you an **equity holder**. But unlike common shareholders' dividends, which only are paid upon profitability, preferred shareholders' dividends are paid out of the company's cash flow instead.

Preferred dividends are paid according to a prearranged schedule as a fixed dividend, either quarterly or biannually.

Preferred stockholders are paid the same dividend percentage rate according to its prospectus amount every dividend period and MOST IMPORTANTLY those dividend payments do not fluctuate and you the investor know in advance the amount and the day you are to receive the dividend.

Preferred Stock Pays DIVIDENDS

Scheduled Payments

One of the reasons preferred stock is so attractive as an investment is because of dividend income that's paid according to a predetermined schedule; decided at the time of the preferred stock's issuance. The schedule of distributions ("dividends") is displayed on the cover of the issuer's prospectus, or on the Free Writing Prospectus, or FWP, which is basically the deal's term sheet.

What is a Preferred Stock Prospectus?

A prospectus is a document (think of it like a book on the company) required by and filed with the Securities and Exchange Commission (SEC) that provides details about an investment offering for sale to the public. A prospectus is filed for preferred stock offerings. A prospectus is used to help investors make a more informed investment decision.

On the next few pages you will find examples of prospectus pages, to familiarize yourself with what to look for. First, let's look below at the cover of a prospectus for an offering of *Allstate Insurance Corporation*'s **Preferred Stock Series H**. As you will notice as you look down the cover, the second paragraph gives the term of the preferred shares and the dates for the dividend payments. It says:

> "Dividends will be payable in arrears at an annual rate equal to 5.10% on January 15, April 15, July 15 and October 15 of each year, commencing October 15, 2019".

Similar language appears in the company's FWP as well.

Prospectus Supplement to Prospectus Dated April 30, 2018

Allstate.

You're in good hands.

The Allstate Corporation

46,000,000 Depositary Shares

Each representing a 1/1,000th Interest in a Share of Fixed Rate
Noncumulative Perpetual Preferred Stock, Series H

Each of the 46,000,000 depositary shares offered hereby (the "Depositary Shares") represents a 1/1,000th interest in a share of Fixed Rate Noncumulative Perpetual Preferred Stock, Series H, $1,00 per value per share, with a liquidation preference of $25,000 per share (equivalent to $25 per Depositary Share) (the "Preferred Stock"), of The Allstate Corporation, deposited with Equiniti Trust Company, as depositary (the "Depositary"). The Depositary Shares are evidenced by depositary receipts. As a holder of Depositary Shares, you are entitled to all proportional rights and preferences of the Preferred Stock, including dividend, voting, redemption and liquidation rights. You must exercise these rights through the Depositary.

We will pay dividends on the Preferred Stock on a noncumulative basis only when, as and if declared by our board of directors (or a duly authorized committee of the board) and to the extent that we have legally available funds to pay dividends. Dividends will accrue from August 8, 2019 on the liquidation amount of $25,000 per share of the Preferred Stock and be payable in arrears at an annual rate equal to 5.10% on January 15, April 15, July 15 and October 15 of each year, commencing October 15, 2019. Dividends on the Preferred Stock are not cumulative. Accordingly, in the event dividends are not declared on the Preferred Stock for payment on any dividend payment date, then those dividends will cease to accrue and cease to be payable. If we have not declared a dividend before the dividend payment date for any dividend period, we will have no obligation to pay dividends accrued for that dividend period, whether or not dividends on the Preferred Stock are declared for any future dividend period.

We may, at our option, redeem the shares of Preferred Stock (i) in whole but not in part at any time prior to October 15, 2024, within 90 days after the occurrence of a "rating agency event" at a redemption price equal to $25,500 per share (equivalent to $25.50 per Depositary Share), plus any declared and unpaid dividends, without regard to any undeclared dividends, (ii) but excluding, the redemption date, or (iii) (a) in whole but not in part at any time prior to October 15, 2024, within 90 days after the occurrence of a "regulatory capital event," or (b) in whole or in part, from time to time, on any dividend payment date on or after October 15, 2024, in each case, at a redemption price equal to $25,000 per share (equivalent to $25 per Depositary Share), plus, in each case, any declared and unpaid dividends, without regard to any undeclared dividends, to, but excluding, the redemption date. If we redeem the Preferred Stock, the Depositary will redeem a proportionate number of Depositary Shares. Neither you, as a holder of Depositary Shares, nor the Depositary will have the right to require the redemption or repurchase of the Preferred Stock or the Depositary Shares.

The Preferred Stock will not have any voting rights except as described in this prospectus supplement.

Investing in the Depositary Shares and the underlying Preferred Stock involves risks. See a discussion of certain risks in the "Risk Factors" section beginning on page S-10 of this prospectus supplement and the periodic reports we file with the Securities and Exchange Commission that should be carefully considered before investing in the Depositary Shares and the underlying Preferred Stock.

Neither the Securities and Exchange Commission nor any other regulatory body has approved or disapproved of these securities or passed upon the accuracy or adequacy of this prospectus supplement or the accompanying prospectus. Any representation to the contrary is a criminal offense.

	Per Depositary Share	Total
Public offering price(1)	$25.0000	$1,150,000,000
Underwriting discount(2)	$0.5715	$26,287,812
Proceeds, before expenses, to The Allstate Corporation(1)	$24.4285	$1,123,712,188

(1) The public offering price set forth above does not include accrued dividends, if any, that may be declared. Dividends, if declared, will accrue from August 8, 2019.

(2) Reflects 27,512,208 Depositary Shares sold to retail investors, for which the underwriters will receive an underwriting discount of $0.7875 per Depositary Share, and 18,487,792 Depositary Shares sold to institutional investors, for which the underwriters will receive an underwriting discount of $0.2500 per Depositary Share.

Application will be made to list the Depositary Shares on the New York Stock Exchange under the symbol "ALL PR H". If the application is approved, trading of the Depositary Shares on the New York Stock Exchange is expected to commence within 30 days after the initial delivery of the Depositary Shares.

The underwriters expect to deliver the Depositary Shares through the facilities of The Depository Trust Company ("DTC") for the accounts of its participants, including Clearstream Banking, S. A. and Euroclear Bank SA/NV, against payment in New York, New York on or about August 8, 2019.

Figure 5

39

Allstate

You're in good hands.

THE ALLSTATE CORPORATION

46,000,000 DEPOSITARY SHARES EACH REPRESENTING A 1/1,000TH INTEREST IN A SHARE OF FIXED RATE NONCUMULATIVE PERPETUAL PREFERRED STOCK, SERIES H

FINAL TERM SHEET

Dated August 1, 2019

Issuer: The Allstate Corporation

Security Type: Depositary shares (the "Depositary Shares") each representing a 1/1,000th interest in a share of Fixed Rate Noncumulative Perpetual Preferred Stock, Series H, of the Issuer (the "Preferred Stock")

Expected Ratings:* Baa2 (Moody's) / BBB (S&P)

Format: SEC Registered

Size: $1,150,000,000 (46,000,000 Depositary Shares)

Liquidation Preference: $25,000 per share of Preferred Stock (equivalent of $25 per Depositary Share)

Term: Perpetual

Dividend Rate (Noncumulative): 5.10% per annum, only when, as and if declared

Dividend Payment Dates: Quarterly in arrears on January 15, April 15, July 15 and October 15 of each year, commencing on October 15, 2019

Trade Date: August 1, 2019

Settlement Date: August 8, 2019 (T+5)

Optional Redemption: The Issuer may, at its option, redeem the shares of Preferred Stock (i) in whole but not in part at any time prior to October 15, 2024, within 90 days after the occurrence of a "rating agency event" at a redemption price equal to $25,500 per share (equivalent to $25.50 per Depositary Share), plus any declared and unpaid dividends, without regard to any undeclared dividends, to, but excluding, the redemption date, or (ii) (a) in whole but not in part at any time prior to October 15, 2024, within 90 days after the occurrence of a "regulatory capital event," or (b) in whole or in part, from time to time, on any dividend payment date on or after October 15, 2024, in each case, at a redemption price equal to $25,000 per share (equivalent to $25 per Depositary Share), plus any declared and unpaid dividends, without regard to any undeclared dividends, to, but excluding, the redemption date.

Listing: Application will be made to list the Depositary Shares on the New York Stock Exchange (the "NYSE") under the symbol

Figure 6

41

When a Dividend Is Not Paid

Just because a company says in its documents it's going to pay dividends on the dates stated, it does not mean that the company always will. Circumstances can arise whereby a dividend is missed or unpaid.

What can you do?

And what if the issuer cannot or does not want to pay a dividend payment?

That's where *Cumulative* vs *Non-Cumulative Preferred Stock* comes into play. If you want to get paid when things go wrong, it is paramount to know the distinction.

Cumulative vs Non-Cumulative Preferred Stock

What is 'Cumulative' Preferred Stock?

Cumulative preferred stock is preferred stock that pays the stockholder whether or not a dividend or multiple dividends are missed. If any dividend payments are missed, for any reason, those missed dividends will accumulate as unpaid and be owing to the preferred stockholder.

These accumulated dividends **must be paid out first to the cumulative preferred shareholders** before any other dividends are ever paid again to shareholders including common shareholders.

Because of this distinction cumulative preferred stock is more desirable than non-cumulative, which does not accumulate if a payment is missed. That being said whenever possible you want to own cumulative preferred for obvious reasons.

What is 'Non-Cumulative' Preferred Stock?

Non-cumulative preferred stock is a type of preferred stock that does not pay the stockholder if one dividend or multiple dividends are skipped or omitted entirely.

It is important to note that an issuer of non-cumulative preferred stock may skip one dividend or all dividends without any penalty as long as the issuer's board gives approval. This means that if an issuer chooses not to pay for any reason, the holder has no rights to claim those unpaid dividends in the future. None. Nada.

Companies may elect to stop paying dividends because of hardship, while others might have different reasons. Regardless of reason, always keep in mind that a non-cumulative preferred can and may just skip a dividend payment whenever they like or need to. All it takes is board approval to stop paying dividends and you are out of luck.

Usually this occurs only because of an extreme situation. The ability to skip or not pay dividends is why buying cumulative preferred shares are more attractive than non-cumulative preferred shares. Keep in mind that once a company skips dividend payments it becomes much harder to find new financing as new investors would be fearful to invest. So, it's not something they do willy-nilly.

Why Would A Dividend Not Be Paid?

The main reason dividends are not paid is because the issuer does not have the money or cannot meet all its financial obligations. When this occurs, the issuer will often choose to 'suspend' its' dividend payments to focus on paying certain expenses and debt payments first. If the issuer is successful getting through its problems and resumes paying dividends again, all holders of cumulative preferred stock are paid first, getting all their dividend payments owed in arrears. All other stockholders must wait until all cumulative preferred dividends are paid and the quarterly preferred stock payment is made before they may receive any dividend payment.

Because all cumulative preferred shareholders must be paid first, a cumulative feature reduces the risk to the investor. Because risk is reduced, cumulative preferred stock sometimes is offered at a lower coupon rate than non-cumulative preferred stock.

Generally, only the strongest companies with long dividend histories issue cumulative preferred stock making them more desirable to us.

How to Know if a Preferred is Cumulative or Non-Cumulative?

It's easy! All you need to do is read the header on the front page of the preferred stock prospectus.

For example:

Allstate.

You're in good hands.

The Allstate Corporation

46,000,000 Depositary Shares
Each representing a 1/1,000th Interest in a Share of Fixed Rate
Noncumulative Perpetual Preferred Stock, Series H

Figure 7

As you can see here, 'Noncumulative Preferred Share Series H' is stated.

This brings me on to something else that Marvin really stressed to me from the beginning: the IMPORTANCE of the PROSPECTUS.

Why the Prospectus is Important

Companies that wish to offer preferred stock for sale to the public must file a prospectus with the SEC. More than that, they must file a preliminary and a final prospectus.

The preliminary prospectus is the first offering document provided by a security issuer and includes most of the details of the business and transaction. However, the preliminary prospectus doesn't contain the number of shares to be issued or price information. Typically, the preliminary prospectus is used to gauge interest in the market for the security being proposed. It 'tests the water'!

The final prospectus contains the **complete details** of the investment offering to the public. The final prospectus contains any finalized background information as well as the number of shares to be issued and the offering price.

A prospectus will include the following crucial information:

- A brief summary of the company's background and financial information.
- The name of the company issuing the stock.

44

- The number of shares.
- Type of securities being offered.
- Names of the company's principals.
- Names of the banks or financial companies performing the underwriting.

Free Writing Prospectus or the FWP

The FWP is a quick snapshot of what the basic information you need to know about buying a new preferred issue. Think of it as your cheat sheet.

For an example turn back to the second ALLSTATE example on page 40. As you can see from that example, ALLSTATE is selling a 5.10% preferred at $25 per share. The shares may be redeemed on or after October 15, 2024.

The DEFINITION of a free writing prospectus is any written communication that is:

- an offer to sell or a solicitation of an offer to buy SEC-registered securities that is used after the registration statement for an offering is filed regardless if a registration statement has or has not been filed.
- made by means other than: a statutory prospectus (a final prospectus, a preliminary prospectus or certain other categories of prospectus that meet the requirements of Section 10(a) (15 U.S.C. § 77j(a)) of the Securities Act);
- a written communication used in reliance on Rule 167 (17 C.F.R. § 230.167) and Rule 426 (17 C.F.R. § 230.426) under the Securities Act (special rules for issuers of asset-backed securities); or
- a communication that is given together with or after delivery of a final prospectus (which therefore falls into the exception from the definition of prospectus in Section 2(a)(10)(a) (15 U.S.C. § 77b(a)(10)(a)) of the Securities Act).

The term free writing prospectus is defined in Rule 405 (17 C.F.R. § 230.405) under the Securities Act.

9

VARIETIES OF PREFERRED STOCK

PREFERRED SHARES, LIKE ICE cream, come in many different flavors. I like vanilla ice cream, Marvin likes mint chocolate chip. We can choose whatever flavor ice cream we like, intolerances aside, without researching the ingredients and history. We have to be more clued-up though when we are choosing our **primary type** of preferred shares. Most preferred shares are one or more forms of the following five primary types:

- Traditional Preferred
- Trust Preferred
- Third Party Trust Preferred
- Convertible Preferred
- Fixed-to-Float Preferred

Throughout the years, different varieties of preferred stock have been created plainly for marketing the securities. As the world of preferred stocks has grown, investment bankers have had to become creative in order to ensure a complete sale of their securities.

Today gimmicks are often used for lesser known or riskier issues.

Some preferred companies have no history. Others lose money.

Each has a different need.

Some gimmicks found in newer preferred shares we find issued today have shorter maturity periods; with some being only two years. Others offer higher yield. **The pitch behind shorter maturity and higher yield is you get paid more for waiting less time to maturity.**

Sounds good – but remember that these **types** often carry **greater risk**. Others are callable in less than the normal five years.

Whatever the gimmick, most vary based on some form of one of these five types of preferred stocks.

Traditional Preferred

Most preferred stocks issued today are traditional preferred. They have a $25 par and redemption at par. They are callable within five-years, others are callable in less. Preferred stock pays a fixed rate dividend which is paid to the holder.

Trust Preferred Stocks (TRUPS)

A trust-preferred security is a security possessing characteristics of both equity and debt.

A company creates a TRUPS by creating a trust, issuing debt to it, and then having it issue preferred stock to investors.

Trust-preferred securities are generally issued by bank holding companies. Because of this setup a TRUPS, unlike traditional preferred stock, is tax deductible by the issuing company *as interest* off the issuing company's taxes.

The TRUPS was a favorite of financial institutions until 2010 when the law changed. You see before 2010, banks found that issuing TRUPS was a great way to raise lots of money, billions of dollars, that could be applied to what's known as "Tier 1 capital" (or the amount of money they needed to have to be in compliance with the banks required capital reserves.) TRUPS basically kept the regulators away with these large reserves.

But that all changed after the financial collapse and regulators started looking to strengthen the banking system. The regulators argued, rightly so, that since TRUPS in their terms provided for **cumulative** dividends (see previous chapter for definition of 'cumulative' vs. 'non-cumulative') that ultimately shareholders had a claim to the money.

As a way to prevent any claims to cash, The *Wall Street Reform Act* no longer allows new cumulative preferred shares to be applied towards Tier 1 capital reserves.

Today almost all bank preferred shares are issued as **non-cumulative** for this very reason, meaning that should the bank skip a payment they do not owe it to you, and that's why it can be applied to Tier 1 capital. As for the TRUPS, once this regulation was enacted TRUPS became dinosaurs and are practically extinct. Several remain trading but in the next few years expect for all of them to disappear.

Third Party Trust Preferred

Create a trust like TRUPS, from whom you purchase your preferred shares, but *instead of the trust being structured to give a **tax benefit** to the issuing company*, the third-party trust **is created to generate a profit to the issuer**.

A profit?

Yes, a profit. Most are issued by brokerage firms who sell you their preferred stock. The brokerage firm, then goes and buys either debt securities or other preferred stock, issued by a third party (or 'third party trust preferred') in the open market. These securities are then sold to the trust to back up the preferred stock that you bought but at a markup over the purchase price they paid in the open market. All this is a way for the brokerage firm to lock in a profit by buying other high-quality preferred shares and other debt and reselling the preferred shares to you at a profit.

Exchange Traded Debt Securities (ETDS)

You must know *The Duck* Test?

If it looks like a duck, swims like a duck, and quacks like a duck, then it probably is a duck.

This reasoning implies that an unknown subject can be identified by observing that subject's characteristics. Additionally, it may also be used to argue that something is not what it appears to be regardless of similarity.

Well, this applies to Exchange Traded Debt Securities or ETDS which is *not preferred stock at all* although they are very similar.

Both pay quarterly coupon payments, have a $25 par value, pay comparable returns to preferred stock and are callable after 5 years BUT they differ in that ETDS are actually bonds (often called "baby bonds").

ETDS are listed on the issuers books as debt rather than equity. As such ETDS pay interest income, not dividends. Unlike most bonds ETDS don't trade on a bond exchange instead they trade on a stock exchange with a stock symbol. Brokerages mistake these securities as preferred stock all the time. Keep in mind this important fact, as this might look like a duck, but ETDS are actually a superior security to preferred stocks and offer lower risk. As a form of bond EDTS have a stronger rating than preferred stock as they also have a higher standing in the issuer's capital structure. Higher standing means more likely to be paid on default. As preferred stock is "preferred" to common stock, bondholders sit higher than preferred making them safer as they would get paid ahead of a preferred holder in liquidation.

Convertible Preferred

Convertible preferred stock is a preferred stock that can be changed into common shares of the underlying issuing company.

Shares are often convertible based upon a conversion ratio specified in the issuing company's prospectus. Typically for each share of convertible preferred stock you own, you will receive a certain number of shares in the company's common stock **upon conversion**.

The conversion ratio and the timing of the conversion is up to you as the owner, unless the company calls for something called '**mandatory conversion**'. Mandatory conversion is when you are forced to convert your shares to common shares according to the conversion ratio set in the prospectus.

While a 'convertible preferred' sounds enticing there are usually more pitfalls than advantages. The major pitfall of convertible preferred is the unknown. As we know, a convertible preferred has some sort of conversion ratio associated with the security. *What we do not know* is what the price of the common stock that the preferred is destined to be converted into will be **in the future**... and this is where the trouble begins.

Yes of course there could be an advantage if the conversion feature was in your favor, but, more often than not, the conversion feature works in favor of the issuing company. Why? Because the issuer has baked into the prospectus provisions to prevent the holder from getting 'too good a deal'.

Some convertibles even have provisions that actually make the deal worse if the deal becomes too good for the holder.

Remember, much of the time the conversion is controlled by the holder but at times, as will be mentioned in the prospectus, the issuer can be forced to convert in a mandatory conversion and once those convertible preferred shares are forced to convert into common stock you may be able to sell them at a profit in the open market or at a loss. Since no one knows the future that's the risk.

Also, after conversion into common shares you no longer have the advantage of being a "preferred" holder. Besides moving down the corporate capital structure to a common stockholder, you are now **last in line** to get dividends on the common stock, if the common stock even pays a dividend.

The reality of owning convertible preferred is that unless the conditions are locked in and somewhat fair, it's best to avoid these altogether as they are risky, and as Marvin says, "we do **not** like risk."

Fixed-to-Float

Fixed-to-Float preferred shares are the "new hot thing" in preferred stock because as rates rise, Fixed-to-Float perpetuals can provide the possibility of higher dividend payments and greater price stability… as the coupon resets **reflecting those new higher rates**.

Fixed-to-Float preferred shares are different from traditional preferred in that they are a sort of hybrid security. Initially, Fixed-to-Float preferred stock starts its life carrying a fixed dividend rate at issuance for a period of time, usually five years but some are seven or ten years. After that period, they become callable by the issuer any time upon 30-days' notice. If the issuer doesn't exercise the call option, the preferred issue's dividend rate will begin to float and reset for as long as the issue remains outstanding as **cited in the company's prospectus**.

Typically, the new dividend rate begins floating, based on a Three-Month LIBOR (The London InterBank Offered Rate) plus somewhere in the range of 3% to 6% (as noted, again, in the prospectus.)

LIBOR rates are published daily in the *Wall Street Journal*, or can be found online at this link from *Bank Rate*:

https://www.bankrate.com/rates/interest-rates/libor.aspx.

See example on the next page…

LIBOR, other interest rate indexes

The LIBOR is among the most common of benchmark interest rate indexes used to make adjustments to adjustable rate mortgages. This page also lists some other less-common indexes.

Click on the links below to find a fuller explanation of the term.

LIBOR, other interest rate indexes   UPDATED: 12/17/2019

	THIS WEEK	MONTH AGO	YEAR AGO
Bond Buyer's 20 bond index	2.74	2.85	4.18
FNMA 30 yr Mtg Com del 60 days	3.32	3.31	4.27
1 Month LIBOR Rate	1.76	1.72	2.47
3 Month LIBOR Rate	1.90	1.89	2.79
6 Month LIBOR Rate	1.90	1.91	2.88
Call Money	3.50	3.50	4.00
1 Year LIBOR Rate	1.97	1.94	3.06

Figure 8 www.bankrate.com (screenshot)

These adjustments to the dividend can be quarterly or semiannual depending on the issue.

Now keep in mind that although Fixed-to-Float securities are usually offered during times of rising rates, there is the real potential for the coupon rate to reset *lower* in a declining rate environment. If LIBOR goes down, that's also a risk.

Let's look at a recent issue.

CAI International (NYSE: CAI-A)

8.50% Series A Fixed-to-Floating Rate

Cumulative Redeemable Perpetual Preferred Stock

Qualified fixed dividend rate 8.50% before 04/15/2023 then switching to paying a floating rate dividend at a rate of the 3-month LIBOR plus a spread of 5.82%

Today's Fixed-to-Float securities are mostly dominated by financial companies and usually issued in initial increments of $25 par or $1000 par. This can be credited to the implementation of the *Dodd-Frank Wall Street and Consumer Protection Act* allowing for the issuing financial institution to use the investment as Tier 1 capital. Tier 1 capital is the core measure of a bank's financial strength from a regulator's perspective. It is composed of core capital, which is common stock, disclosed reserves and non-redeemable non-cumulative preferred stock. Non-cumulative here is important to understand as Fixed-to-Float dividends paid by banks are not obligated to make up any missed payments, should they occur.

10

WHY CORPORATIONS SELL PREFERRED STOCK

MARVIN, I UNDERSTAND WHY investors would want to invest in preferred shares, as they pay the most in the fixed income space and most are large established companies... but **why do companies sell preferred shares that pay so much?**"

Marvin replied, "to raise huge sums of money".

He went on, "what most people don't realize is just how *much* money. We are talking about raising hundreds of millions or even billions of dollars in a single shot."

"Billions! Why?"

"Because even though preferred stock acts like a bond, in that it pays a steady quarterly payment, it is still a stock and is still equity on the company's books."

"What does that mean?" I asked him.

"It means that the preferred stock sold to raise those billions of dollars goes on a corporation's books not as debt, but *as equity* instead!

Preferred stock sold to raise money does not hit the company's debt load! And as a company's **debt-to-equity ratio** is one of the most common metrics used to analyze the financial stability of a business the lower the number is, the more attractive the business appears to investors. Selling preferred stocks keeps that number low."

"That's some trick!" I said.

Marvin continued, "Remember, too many bonds issued by a company can be a red flag for potential investors because the strict schedule of debt repayments for obligations must be adhered to, no matter what the company's financial circumstances are… unlike with preferred shares which can *uniquely* skip or defer payments because they have flexibility."

"Yes! So, you're saying that since the preferred shares are not obligated or forced to make a dividend payment and the sale of preferred doesn't hit the debt-to-equity ratio that's a main reason company's sell preferred."

"Yes, also they can raise tons of money and not give up voting rights to those shares as well. That being said, a company can issue large amounts of preferred stock without altering control of the public company."

Preferred Stock Gives Corporations Flexibility Compared to Bonds

It's true what Marvin said: preferred stocks do not follow the same guidelines of debt repayment because they are equity issues. With a preferred stock these dividend payments may be deferred by the company – or skipped in their entirety – if the company falls into financial hardship. (We will discuss how, as an investor, you can avoid this later.) This feature of preferred stock offers maximum flexibility to the company without the fear of missing or making a debt dividend payment. Unlike bond issues, a missed payment puts the company at risk of defaulting on an issue, and that could result in forced bankruptcy.

Corporations also like preferred shares for their call feature. (Most, but not all, preferred stock is callable). After a set date, the issuer can call the shares at par value to refinance at a lower rate if rates have dropped. This gives the company great flexibility to refinance debt over a short period as rates decline.

Why Do Banks Issue Preferred When They Can Borrow Using Bonds at Lower Rates?

"Everything you are saying makes sense, Marvin, but what I cannot get my head around is, why would a bank issue a 6% preferred share that pays a 6% dividend when the bank can lend to a person for a mortgage at only 4%? Also, banks today are taking in money to pay CD's whereby the bank pays 1.75% on money they borrow; so why would they pay 6% to a preferred stockholder? I don't understand.

"What I am asking is, why would a bank want to issue preferred shares for upwards of double the coupon rate compared to bonds? Also why do so many banks issue preferred?"

Marvin looked unfazed, "The answer," he said, "is in the details on this one. Let's start with Tier 1 capital."

Tier 1 Capital

"As you already know banks are heavily regulated. One thing that regulators care about is that the bank is able to meet the capital ratio set, or Tier 1 capital.

Big banks need huge money to support liabilities. To meet those giant liabilities, banks issue mounds of non-cumulative preferred shares to meet that required capital ratio.

Why?

Because issuing non-cumulative preferred shares doesn't require dividend payments to be paid and also avoids *common ownership dilution* as the shares are **non-voting**. This is why the preferred market is filled with banks and financial institution types, who use the shares to have adequate Tier 1 capital.

Note that the *Dodd-Frank Act* phased out cumulative preferred and trust preferred securities within Tier 1 capital status.[6]"

Certain Preferred Shares Stay Off Balance Sheet

"Banks also love preferred because it stays off the balance sheet.

Think, how do you stay a low-debt-to-equity company?

Or how can you take in lots of capital that is not shown as debt on your balance sheet?

Easy, issue preferred rather than issue debt.

It's tricky I know, but remember preferred stock is **stock** not **debt**. That is key because it is listed as such on the company's books. Preferred stock, unlike bonds, gives banks flexibility in making their dividend payments. As with other corporations, if a bank is running into cash issues, it can suspend

---

[6] Source: United States. Office of the Comptroller of the Currency, Treasury; and the Board of Governors of the Federal Reserve System. 2013. "Regulatory Capital Rules: Regulatory Capital, Implementation of Basel III, Capital Adequacy, Transition Provisions, Prompt Corrective Action, Standardized Approach for Risk-weighted Assets, Market Discipline and Disclosure Requirements, Advanced Approaches Risk-Based Capital Rule, and Market Risk Capital Rule."

preferred dividend payments without risk of default which differs from bonds. You cannot do that with bonds. If bank bonds miss a payment that could put them into technical default, which could trigger a host of things including an immediate call on previously issued bonds or an increase interest rates on those bonds. A technical default may also occur when the debt-to-equity ratio breaches a limit set in a currently issued bond covenant.

Raising money using preferred stock **avoids this scenario** as preferred stock is not listed as debt on the bank's books."

'Poison Pill'

"Finally, some preferred shares act as something called a "poison pill". A poison pill is a financial tactic used by a company to make an unwanted takeover prohibitively expensive or less desirable. In the event of a hostile takeover, some preferred shares contain a provision that forces the preferred stock to be 'called' during a change in control, requiring the suitor to come up with a larger amount of cash to acquire the target."

"I get it! Banks use preferred to get lots of money, keep control, and keep their debt to equity ratio low. Pretty smart!"

Now let's talk why underwriters sell investors preferred stock and how preferred stock itself works."

Why Underwriters Sell Preferred

The Underwriters' Incentive? Lots and Lots of Money

The market for preferred stock over the last decade has grown dramatically.

Why?

One word - profit!

It's a money-maker for the underwriter. Preferred stock sales are a risky venture to the issuer, but they come with an enormous profit to that underwriter once sold.

How big? Can you say huge?

The smaller issues brought to market routinely contain a $5 to $10 million-dollar commission and the larger issues on a larger sale could be as large as, get this, $45 to $90 million dollars! That's right! That's just one offering completed. As unbelievable as it may seem that's how much the underwriters are paid. Routinely the commission paid is 3% of the gross offering.

So how do we know this? Easy, it's posted right on the cover of every prospectus cleverly disguised as something called the **underwriting discount**.

So, what's the underwriting discount? Also known as underwriting commission, it is a percentage of the offering price for equity or a percentage of the principal amount of debt that constitutes the compensation paid to the underwriters for marketing and selling the offering.

Again, there is no fixed amount but routinely that number is around 3%. Larger companies (*Fortune 500* types) can usually negotiate lower than 3% if they feel the sale will not be difficult.

Consider a recent offering for *Duke Energy*.

On this offering the commission to the underwriter was $27,758,069.62 on a $1,000,000,000 raise or 2.775%. Not a bad day. *Duke* is currently ranked 125th on the *Fortune 500* list.

With this issue, the underwriters are taking in $27,000,000+ in commission! Keep that in mind. The sale of preferred shares is a business and a profitable one at that.

Clearly, *Duke Energy* is a reputable company and is highly rated with credit agencies, but would well-known underwriters, underwrite other deals that are not as reputable or creditworthy? The answer sadly is yes. Think about it this way. What would *you* do to make $27,000,000 with one quick sale? That is how underwriters and investment bankers think too. So, remember that despite an underwriter's reputation they still may not have your best interest at heart. It happens every day. This is a primary reason we are seeing a new crop of dicier and dicier issuers with much greater risk entering the preferred stock pool.

11

GRAVITY
& 'HOW CALL DATES WORK'

A S WE HAVE LEARNED, preferred stock trades just like a common stock on an exchange and pays a fixed dividend. The shares of preferred stock are sold by the issuer at values of generally $25, $50, $100 or $1,000 per share. Those shares can be bought back by the issuer known as "being called" for the amount they sold for originally. Normally the "call date" is five years from the date of original issuance. In other words, on the call date, the company can choose to buy the shares back or leave them trading and paying the dividend forever or until the maturity date if they have one. Most preferred shares have a maturity date that is 25-50 years into the future. Others have no maturity date at all and are called **'perpetual'** meaning they never ever have to be repurchased. The call date is one of the greatest distinctions between preferred and common stock and the most important. The call date works for both the issuing company and the investor equally.

For the issuer, it is a great way to keep control of financing costs as the call feature allows the issuer to call or buy back the preferred shares at times when interest rates have declined.

What the preferred issuer will do is buy the existing preferred shares back and then issue brand new preferred shares **at a lower dividend rate**.

For instance, if a preferred share issued five years ago was paying a 6.25%

dividend but now rates have dropped to a place whereby the issuer can replace those shares with a new 5.50% preferred stock the issuer will do that, saving themselves 0.75%. This saving might seem insignificant until you look at a $500 million dollar offering:

The 0.75% savings on a $500 million preferred alone is $3,750,000 a year or $18,750,000 over 5 years alone.

Truly everything counts in large amounts with preferred stock and dividend rates.

Now the issuer isn't the only one who benefits from a preferred stock being called. The investor too has benefits.

The Reactive Way Preferred Stock Trades

While common stock and preferred stock look similar, the two couldn't be more different. Yes, daily prices of both common and preferred stock may similarly vary from minute-to-minute, day-to-day week-to-week but that's where the similarity ends.

Common stock by nature is rudderless and may trade in any direction, for any reason. Conversely, preferred stock is guided by rules originally outlined in its prospectus which often **nudge the shares in a specific direction at a specific time**. Preferred stock is guided by a few guiding principles.

- Gravity
- Call Date Gravity
- Maturity Date Gravity
- Investor Trading

Gravity

Gravity, by definition, is the force by which a body draws objects toward its center. The force of gravity keeps all of the planets in orbit around the sun. Gravity is also the natural force that causes things to fall toward the earth.

Similarly, **preferred shares have their own gravity** which cause the preferred share prices to move back towards their original offering price, or par.

When a new preferred is issued, the prospectus provides the buyer with key dates and dividend information. This information includes the call date and the maturity date as well as the dividend rate and the day each quarter when the dividend is to be issued.

These dates are paramount in understanding how a preferred share will behave and react to gravity.

Call Date Gravity

Let's start with the call date. Once a preferred is issued the call date or the redeem date, a fixed date usually five years into the future, becomes the first time the issuing company can buy back all the shares at par, the original issuance price. This date is public knowledge and every buyer in the preferred space will know this call date.

Now, if the issuer were to call the preferred on the call date, the company must pay you par or what the security sold for when it was first issued (sold for) on that call date. If the par was $25 when issued, you will get $25 per share when redeemed/called.

Example:

So, it is four years and ten months since the preferred share was first issued at $25. The five-year mark to call or be redeemed is approaching. Rates have dropped and it looks like the issuer of the preferred stock is going to call the security. The stock is now trading at $25.75 per share. As the call date approaches, what do you guess will happen to the price of the trading preferred stock, in the market, if there is a likely chance that the preferred will in fact be called? The answer is the preferred shares in advance of the call date will start moving back down towards the $25 price. Why? Gravity! The shares will be pulled towards the original issue price because that's the amount you will be paid from the issuer and since no one else will pay you more if the shares are going to all be bought back at par this will lead all the outstanding trading shares of that issuance of that preferred to trade right around par in this case $25.

But what if the shares are trading lower than $25? Does gravity apply?

Yes! It does not matter what price the shares are trading at as they will be bought from you automatically at $25 or par (in this example) on the call date.

In this scenario instead of moving down from a higher price the shares will move up from the lower price to the original issuance price.

Gravity buoyancy.

Keep in mind that the issuer does not have to buy your shares back when the call date approaches. The issuer will only call the shares if it is in the best interest of the company where the issuing company can buy back that debt to refinance it at a lower rate. If the company cannot refinance the debt at a lower rate and there is no other pressing reason for the company to buy back those preferred shares, they will not call the preferred.

But if there is even a hint that the shares may possibly be called you will see gravity at work moving the shares towards par. **Do not ignore a movement in share price towards par.** Any thinking that the shares won't be called despite market movement could give you an undesired result. Just like in nature, gravity is a force projecting a direction, don't resist it.

Remember gravity is not just a rule: it's a law.

One last thing. Often the final payment on redemption is slightly more than par because the issuing company still owes you a final partial dividend for the last quarter or days that have accrued since the last dividend was paid. This is called the "accrued distribution" and it is added to the par payment redeemed amount.

The formula to arrive at what they will owe you is this:

Accrued Distribution Formula

Par x Dividend rate % / 360 x the number of days since the last dividend payment - 1 day =

Just add this amount to the par price per share and that is the amount you will receive on redemption.

Example of a $25 par 6% dividend preferred with 30 days since the last dividend.

$$\$25 \times 6\% / 360 \times 30 - 1 = \$0.12 + 25 = \$25.12$$

Maturity Date Gravity

Gravity works the same way on a preferred stock coming to the end of its life at maturity. Regardless of where the stock is trading on the maturity date in the public market, the stock will be purchased at par, as long as the company is solvent and has the financial resources.

The preferred stock on maturity if the company is solvent will be at par. If it's not – beware that something is wrong. Again, gravity will pull the trading price of the preferred shares down or up, whatever the case may be as the maturity date approaches. Why? Like the call date scenario no one is going to pay you more than par at maturity. As a maturity date approaches, you can see how the security behaves in its inching towards par.

Investor Trading

As no one can predict the future, it's anyone's guess how most investments will perform. But, unlike other investments, preferred shares are different. Because of the nature of preferred stock, while we can't exactly predict the future, we can guess how preferred shares may behave and where and when they will trade by looking at its prospectus' terms. Barring unforeseen or extreme situations the predictability of these shares can be made due to the way investors behave *en masse*.

The commonality between buyers and sellers when buying preferred shares can be looked at in three ways.

1. All buyers want to buy preferred shares as low as possible.
2. All sellers of preferred shares want to sell their shares as high as possible.
3. Both buyers and sellers want their dividends sooner than later. After all, if you could get your dividend next week or next month which would *you* prefer?

As we know dividend dates for preferred shares are fixed for years. These fixed dates are great as investors in preferred shares know when they will receive dividends for years. But also knowing dividend dates and ex-dividend dates also influences investors behavior and how preferred shares behave and **react**. Marvin showed me how with this example:

You're new to the preferred stock world. Today you are going to purchase your first preferred shares. To keep this simple, let's say you bought 1,000 shares from your broker at $25 per share and it had a 6% dividend. Again $25 x 6% = $1.50 per share per year as a dividend. If we divide that by 4 quarters, you will receive a dividend of $0.375 ($1.50 / 4 = $0.375) per share per quarter or $375 per quarter total from your 1,000 shares.

It's important to know how much you will receive per quarter as we will see. Being it's the first preferred shares you purchased you are excited and can't wait to get that first dividend in your account. As the date approaches you know you are going to get $0.375 a share or a total $375 dividend.

Now it's the last day before the dividend is to be paid and you are going to get that $0.375 per share or $375 tomorrow, but what if I was to tell you I would pay you $250 today or $0.25 per share, would you take it?

It is not a trick question.

It's $250 today or $375 tomorrow?

Obviously, you would take the $375 tomorrow and so would everyone else.

If I asked you why you wouldn't sell to me for $250 you would say why would I sell to you today for $0.25 a share or $250 when if I just wait one more day and I'll get $375, and that's the point.

The only logical way you would sell to me a day early is for $0.375 or a total of $25.375 per share.

Marvin went on to explain, "understanding this behavior, and that we bought our shares at $25 per share, where do you think the price of the stock should go as the dividend date approaches?

"If you said the stock should move closer to $25.375 to include the dividend being paid you would be correct as the preferred share is still holding onto its bounty and has the dividend to be paid still attached to it.

"Can you guess what will happen to the share price after the dividend is paid?"

"Does the share price decrease?"

"That's correct. Usually the decline is close to the value just dispersed. So, the stock usually moves up towards the dividend date and then down after its dispensed."

"Okay," I pondered. "We know that when we own the shares we get the dividend, but what if I were to sell my shares? Would I still get my dividend?"

Marvin replied, "well that depends as preferred shares have a method for determining that as well.

To avoid any confusion as to who receives the dividend, the securities industry came up with something called the **ex-dividend date**. The name "ex-dividend" is kind of awful and confusing. To make it easier just think of ex-dividend date as the "no-dividend" date or "without-dividend" date."

Here's some further explaining, from me!

What Is the 'Ex-Dividend' (or the 'No Dividend') Date

Ex-dividend describes a stock that is trading without (ex) the value of the next dividend payment.

Ex-dividend = no dividend!

A buyer who purchases a stock on or after the ex-dividend date **is not entitled to the declared dividend** – it is owned by whoever owned the stock the day before the ex-dividend date.

Again, ex-dividend = no dividend!

You buy **on** that date you get no dividend.

You buy **before** that date and hold the security you get the dividend.

The ex-dividend date or **"ex-date"** is usually set one business day before the record date. This bears repeating. *The ex-dividend date for stocks is usually set one business day before the record date!*

Let's be clear. If you want to receive the dividend, on a preferred share that is trading in the market, you must buy or hold that share **one day before** the ex-date. If you buy **on** the ex-date or after, you will not get the dividend.

Last time, to get the dividend we buy one day before the no-dividend date or ex-dividend date.

How the Ex-Dividend Date Affects the Trading Price of Preferred Shares

"Okay, so you got it," nodded Marvin. "Preferred share prices rise in the lead up to the ex-dividend date and fall after the ex-dividend date.

Now that we know "the cutoff date" to buy and get the dividend, we have to realize that **all of Wall Street knows that the same**. Understanding that… what would you assume happens to a **preferred share price** as we get

closer to the ex-date?"

I was pretty proud of my quick answer!

"Do buyers on the street bid up the share price?"

"Correct! As buyers bid up those preferred shares, the price rises alongside to match the additional value those shares carry being the dividend. In our example our $25 share as we move to towards the ex-date will pretty much reflect the dividend up until the day before the ex-date where the price per share will just about reflect the entire dividend. If our quarterly dividend is $0.375 we can expect the last day before the ex-date for the preferred share to now trade at or close to $25.375. **If you want to be a seller of preferred remember the best prices to sell are the days closest, but before the ex-dividend date.**"

Preferred Share Prices Drop on and after the 'Ex-Date'

"What goes up must come down! This is also true of preferred shares and dividends. As bidding drives up the price of preferred shares towards the ex-dividend date, what do you think happens to the preferred share price once the dividend payment is given to the holder and the ex-date begins without a dividend? If you guess the preferred share price drops or goes down, you are correct. Once the value has been given away, typically the preferred share gives up a value equal or similar to the amount of dividend just paid. It happens like clockwork.

"Looking at our example. Our $25 preferred share has increased to $25.375 over time leading up to the day before the ex-dividend date. The next day which is the ex-date we can almost predict with some certainty that the preferred share will go down in an amount similar to amount of dividend paid or down $0.375. So, on the ex-date we could expect the preferred share to go from the $25.375 down towards $25."

Let's look at a preferred movement for Annaly Capital Management Inc. Pfd. Series I (NLY-I) in action!

Annaly Capital issued this new 6.75% Series I preferred on June 21, 2019. The yearly dividend for this security is $1.6875 ($25 x 6.75% = $1.6875 / 4 = $0.4218) and quarterly dividend is $0.4218.

As a new issue (IPO) buyers in the wholesale market were able buy shares early under par at $24.75. The shares first dividend was set to go ex-dividend on August 30th, 2019, or 60 days later.

In the first 30 days the shares slowly crept up to approximate $25.40 or par plus a retained dividend.

Figure 9

Over the next 30 days the share price crept up further another $0.42 to $25.82 to reflect the $0.42 dividend about to be paid to the preferred holder the day before the ex-date.

The next day on the ex-date, like clockwork, the share price declined from $0.42 to $25.40 reflecting the dividend that was paid to the holder of records pre the ex-date.

Best Days to Buy or Sell

Marvin said, "One of the things to know is that **before** and **on** the 'ex-dividend date' are actually the best days to buy or sell preferred shares as the stock has completed its dividend quarter, with its next dividend to be paid in 90 days."

"So why would I sell?"

"Yes, I get your thinking. If you sell you *will* miss the dividend payment… *but* you will get the best price for the shares you own for the period. If you buy on the ex-date you will have to wait a quarter to get the next dividend but buying on the ex-date gets you the lowest share price, usually for the period."

12

INTEREST RATE FLUCTUATION AND ITS EFFECTS

T HE FACT IS THAT interest rates change over time. Sometimes the changes are small other times the changes are large. Either way interest rates are never totally static. **As a preferred stockholder you can benefit no matter whichever way interest rates go.** Let's look at what happens when interest rates go up and down.

When Interest Rates Go Down...

Market Prices of Higher Dividend Preferred Shares Typically Go Up

One of the most important things to remember about preferred stock is the going interest rate and the market price of preferred shares generally move **in opposing directions.** The main exception is when there is a short period to call remaining or a call to redeem or at maturity where gravity dominates and takes control.

Let's start with a basic example.

Suppose you bought a preferred at $25 per share last year with a 6%

dividend. This year newly issued $25 preferred shares of the same issuer are paying just a 5% dividend.

What do you think could happen to the price of the 6% dividend preferred bought last year, should it have gone up or down?

When dividend rates go down existing preferred shares typically go up.

Why?

The answer is just what you would think it would be:

For the same $25 would you rather have an investment that pays you more or less?

More obviously.

Which would you rather own a 5% or 6% preferred?

The 6% of course.

That being the case the demand for 6% preferred will rise with more buying by the public and so will its stock price.

But where will the price rise to, or stop?

The answer isn't exact but understand that when investors chase yield, *they chase until it stops making sense.*

Think of it like this: for a **6% preferred** to yield the same as a **5% preferred**, the price of the preferred can rise up to $29 a share. We figure this out by taking the dividend from the 6% preferred which is **6% x 25 = $1.50 per year** and then **dividing** that yearly dividend by **$29 per share** to come to 5.17%. **($1.50 / 29 = 5.17%).**

At a 5.17% yield we are pretty close to the yield that you could get in the new 5% $25 preferred.

Let's look at a 'flip side' example, that has rates moving up and prices moving down:

Suppose you bought a 6% preferred at $25 but in this scenario a year later new preferred shares from the same company are selling higher with a $25 preferred share paying a 7% dividend.

Which would you rather own a 6% or 7% preferred?

The 7% of course.

What will likely happen to the 6%, $25 preferred you bought last year, as the demand for the 6% preferred decreases with less buying by the public?

That's right the stock price should move lower as everyone would rather own the $25 preferred paying 7% because it pays more. Accordingly, the 6%, $25 preferred share should move down in price as long as no call is imminent or possible. While we do not know exactly **how low** the 6%, $25 preferred share could go, we **do** know that to obtain **an equivalent** yield of 7% the preferred could possibly go down to **$21 or $25 x 6% = $1.50 dividend per year / $21 = 7.14%.**

13

CANARY IN THE COALMINE
& OTHER METAPHORS

WHEN EXPOSED TO POISONOUS gases, canaries feel ill effects and die faster than humans. That's why coalminers used to bring caged canaries into coal mines."

"So, in effect what you're saying Marvin is that, when the canaries became sick or died **down in the mines**, this was the sign that something was seriously wrong and that the miners needed to get **up and out**?"

"Exactly! It seems cruel to us now. But even so, the phrase 'canary in the coal mine' lives on as a metaphor for any warning of serious danger to come."

"Is there a less emotive metaphor we could use, Marvin? Something more modern?"

"I guess… Absolutely in fact! And it's something we've already discussed. 'Common stock' can be *our* new 'canary'. Let me explain. One interesting point is that canaries weren't inherently prophetic… they needed to taken into the coalmine. So any replacement metaphor would have to be a symbol that is small, innocent, and not prophetic under normal circumstances.

"In the case of preferred stock, the issuer's **normally unprophetic common shares** act as the prophetic canary giving us a free look to the

future and warning of serious danger to come."

"How?"

"As you will remember, no common stockholder can be paid profits/dividends, until all the preferred shareholders are paid. Every quarter, companies that issue preferred shares *who also issued common shares* have to announce whether they intend to pay dividends on those common shares or not.

"In this commonplace scenario the company can do several things. They can raise the dividend, lower the dividend, keep the dividend the same or halt paying a dividend altogether. Whatever the result, it basically demonstrates whether or not the company has enough money on hand to pay dividends to the common shareholders."

"I think I understand. What's the main thing to watch for?"

"If the issuer states it intends to pay a dividend, that means that the preferred shareholders will **definitely be paid**. Even if the dividend is just a penny to the common shareholders that means that all the preferred shareholders will be paid in full."

"But what if the dividend is cancelled?"

"If the dividend goes **unpaid** and/or the future common dividends are **halted** that is the first sign you should have concern. If that happens it's as if the canary in the coal mine has become sick or died and that you, the preferred shareholder, need to get out right away!"

"So, in essence the common shares of an issuer often act as an alert system for the preferred holders as to an issuer's ability to pay. If I see common share dividends being lowered or eliminated altogether it's time to reevaluate my investment in the preferred share."

"Yep. If you have ANY concerns at this point AT ALL, this is the time to sell.

"No common dividend means, the trains coming right at you and you should get off the tracks." He paused, then looked at me. "I know that one's a cruel metaphor too, but please can we let that one stand?"

14

BOOSTING YOUR YIELD

MARVIN'S LESSONS BECAME A little more complex (and also more exciting) from this point on. I suppose one could say that Complexity's Yield Curve moves in tandem with our Engagement and Learning!

In the next part of *The Billionaire's Secret,* you will find out much more about mastering the magic of preferred stock investment, as well as some additional crucial 'cards in the pack': like metrics, key terms, credit ratings and so on. So, these next two chapters are the last in *this* part of the book. And in them, we're going back to consider "yield" from some more angles. Back to Marvin…

"One of the features of owning preferred stock is the ability to boost your dividend yield."

"How?"

"As you've seen, dividends are paid on a **per share** basis, so as the holder you are paid per owned share regardless of where the preferred stock price trades.

"If you own a preferred stock that has a **$25 par** that pays a **6% fixed dividend** you will receive **$1.50 per share** per year, or **$0.375 cents** per quarter."

$25 par x 6% dividend rate = $1.50 per year dividend
$1.50 / 4 = $0.375 per quarter

"As such," Marvin continued, "total dividends paid are based on the number of shares you own. In this scenario if you owned 1,000 shares you would receive $1,500 per year as dividends or 1,000 x $1.50 = $1,500. You will get $1.50 per share (or $1,500) regardless of the trading share price *because the calculation is based on the dividend amount paid and multiplied by the amount of shares you own.*"

"But what happens if the share price changes? Or what if the overall stock market drops due to some event and I'm now able to buy the same $25 preferred share for just $20 per share?"

"As you know the dividend amount paid per share will remain the same, but the **yield** received on your investment… **that will change**. I know you're going to ask why!

"Because when you can buy a share for more or less than $25, **the return on the money you invested**, or your **'yield'**, is actually lower or higher than the 'declared dividend'.

"Again, the dividend is calculated using par which in this case is $25 per share. So, if we use the same 6% dividend scenario on a $25 par share, the shareholder will receive a $1.50 per share dividend regardless whether the price of the share goes to $20 or $30."

"But what if you are able to buy the 6% preferred at just $20 per share or $5 under par in the marketplace?"

"Well then you are getting to buy more return with less money and the result is the yield now grows 7.50%."

"How's that?"

"We take the dividend per share (or $1.50 in this case) to be the constant and divide it by the share price you bought your shares for.

Example

$1.50 divided by $20 gives you a 7.5% yield. So, buying a share at $20 per share boosts the overall return from a 6% per share dividend to a 7.5% yield.

The opposite happens when you buy a preferred share at a price higher than $25. Again, using our 6% $25 par share paying $1.50 per year per share: if we were to buy it for $30 a share, or $5 above par, our yield will go down from a 6% dividend per share to 5% yield. $1.50 divided by $30 is 5%.

Changing Preferred Share Price Creates Opportunity for Profit

"As we all know, interest rates are dynamic. They change. Rates are never entirely static. Sometimes they move with great frequency, other times with little movement. Over a period of time, rates will go up and down. Depending how you position yourself you can profit greatly from the moves **IN EITHER DIRECTION** with both capital gains and in yield.

> "In a nutshell, this is what makes
> 'preferred stock investing' beautiful."

"First let's look at the obvious. When dividend rates decline, typically preferred share prices rise. Normally investors love an increase in share price but with preferred shares that gain is additionally amplified. Yes, a rise from $25 a share to $29 a share is significant. If you were to choose to sell you would have a $4 capital gain per share from $25 to $29 a share, which is 16%, but this capital gain would be before any dividends you might have earned along the way as well. You see, on a $25 preferred share that has a 6% dividend, if you sold the preferred shares after only two quarters you would have received 3% in dividends. If you add this to the 16% in capital gains you could obtain by selling the preferred shares you would earn **a total of 19%**.

"In a nutshell this is what makes preferred stock investing beautiful. The fact that you can get great dividends for holding the shares and when opportunity strikes you can combine it with capital gains, you get fantastic returns. All of this by purchasing some of the most stable and strong companies on Earth. This is just one of the ways preferred shares can earn solid returns of 10-20% a year.

"While the thought of the preferred shares you own going down in price may not be appealing at first glance, this downward movement typically provides a great opportunity. This is the type of opportunity that preferred holders hope for." I thought back to that relaxed atmosphere at breakfast that time, and knew he was speaking truth. However, I had to ask,

"But what if rates moved up, and you are holding a preferred share with a lower dividend than new preferred shares are paying now, then what happens?"

"The quick answer is more than likely your preferred share will go down. A $25 par 6% preferred will likely go down in share price if similar shares come to market for instance at 6 ½% or 7%."

"Okaaaay… so, how low can those preferred shares decline?"

"Now THAT is anyone's guess, but the shares will likely move down eventually to rest at a point where those shares are close to equilibrium in yield with the newly issued preferred stock.

"For an old 6% dividend preferred to compete with a 6 ½% preferred the share price could decline to $X. Which would mean you would be down $X on each share of your investment. I know what you're thinking - that sucks."

"Too right I am! But it doesn't really suck, does it? And you're about to tell me why."

"No, it doesn't suck. And for a few reasons.

"First, if you have a preferred investment, you invested to receive dividends. Regardless if the share price goes up or down, the shares are expected to pay their dividends and if its 6% over five years you can still expect to get your total 30% return. You are going to receive this return barring any extraordinary, unforeseen event and all you need to do is sit back and let the dividends roll in.

"Second, if the price of your preferred stock decreases, that provides **several opportunities**. One opportunity being that it will allow you to average down the price in from what you originally purchased your first round of shares for. For instance, if you bought 1,000 shares at $25 and now you can purchase an additional 1,000 shares for $23 your new average price will be $24. When the shares are called or come to a point where the shares may be called, we will see some of that 'call date gravity'; with the shares floating up back close to $25. Should the shares be called or move back to par at $25 your investment would add another $2,000 in profit (capital gain) when sold back to the traded – being 2,000 shares x $1 in profit = $2,000. This would increase your overall return by an additional 4% – being $2,000 / $50,000 = 4%. The capital gain of $2,000, or 4%, plus the 30% return over five years will **increase that overall return to 34%.** But wait there's more…

"When you average down those shares from $25 to $24 by buying an additional 1,000 shares you have also caused your yield to rise to 6.25% from that point forward as your lower average share price is now $24!

"Take the $25 x 6% =$1.50 per year.

"Now divide that $1.50 by $24 = 6.25%. **That's your yield going forward** because you own shares *below par.* Now let's pretend you averaged those shares down to $24 as shown above after year one. Also let's pretend you took out those dividends. That means going forward your return has gone up 0.25% to 6.25% per year. When you add that 0.25% per year up for the next four years (4 x 0.25% = 1%) to the 34% from the scenario above, we now have a total **35%.** When we take that 35% and divide it over the five-year period (35% / 5 = 7%) you get an average 7% return per year. A year! Not so bad after all.

"The last scenario contains a small decline in the stock price of the $25, 6% preferred. But what would happen if the market had a crash or mini crash and the preferred shares you owned dropped by a huge amount? To answer that, keep in mind that suave preferred investors love a big decline. Professional preferred investors know that a huge decline is the best way to make a fortune on preferred shares. Sure, initially the cost basis you have the shares at is dramatically lower (which is initially frightening), but these types of dramatic downturn have provided enormous opportunities as we will see going forward."

One story Marvin told me totally summed it up perfectly.
I was sitting with him one morning where he seemed down.
It was uncommon for him.
I asked what was going on to which he replied *they called my preferred stock, and I'll never be able to replace it. It has paid me over 30% on my money per year for the last 9 years. My broker keeps telling it's a good day because my capital gain will be over $1.8 million dollars, but I want the income.*

I asked Marvin to tell me the story.

Back in 2008, Deutsche Bank issued an $25 par 8% preferred share. Shortly after issuing it in March 2009 the stock market virtually collapsed. The preferred dropped to a little over $6 per share. The economy was shaky and large investment banks like *Lehman Brothers* and *Bear Stearns* were put out of business or acquired for pennies on the dollar accordingly.

The financial crisis hit hard. The scary part was no one knew if other large financial firms would go out of business, like *Lehman*.

That all changed with a few words.

"Too big to fail."

Once President Obama had said that and pledged the United States government to back stopping the 'too big to fail types', Marvin said he bought as much preferred stock as he could.

Other countries soon after also pledged to keep the banking system afloat. One preferred stock Marvin had invested in was *Deutsche Bank*. "I read in the paper that it was the first time *Deutsche Bank* had taken a loss in 50 years. I felt that *Deutsche* could survive. But more importantly I saw that because of the bank's reputation it was able to raise the additional capital necessary... including the bank's **tier one capital** which had reportedly jumped to 10.1%. I felt the bank had the money to stay alive. At that point I was all in. I bought the best preferred share I could buy. All the big names.

"But this *Deutsche* was the one where I was able to get the highest yield. I bought 100,000 shares at an average of $6.35 a share for $635,000. At $6.35 a share the yield was about 31.5% alone. So, get this, every year on my $635,000 investment I would get my $2 dividend per share or $2 x 100,000 shares or $200,000. This went on for nine years.

"When in late 2018 the issue was finally called at par of $25. The long-term capital gain was $1,865,000 on call. Altogether, the nine years of dividends yielding 31.5% earned me (9 years x $200,000 per year =) $1.8 million. When you add that to the capital gain of $1,865,000, it **totaled $3,665,000**, not bad for a **$635,000 investment**." But, he continued, he was still sad because he wouldn't live long enough to replicate it.

A similar example from 2009 that still trades today from *Deutsche Bank* is symbol **DKT Deutsche Bank Contingent Capital Trust 8.05%**. Similarly, in March 2009 this security dropped to trade in the mid $9 per share range. Investors who bought theses shares in 2009 at $9.50 were able to achieve a yield of 21% or $2.01 per year per each share of DKT owned. As the stock currently trades at $25.63 the capital gain available now per share is $16.13 per share and dividends earned for the last ten years total $20. Per each $9.50 share purchased, the return has been $36.13 per share or approximately a total return of 380%. (See below)

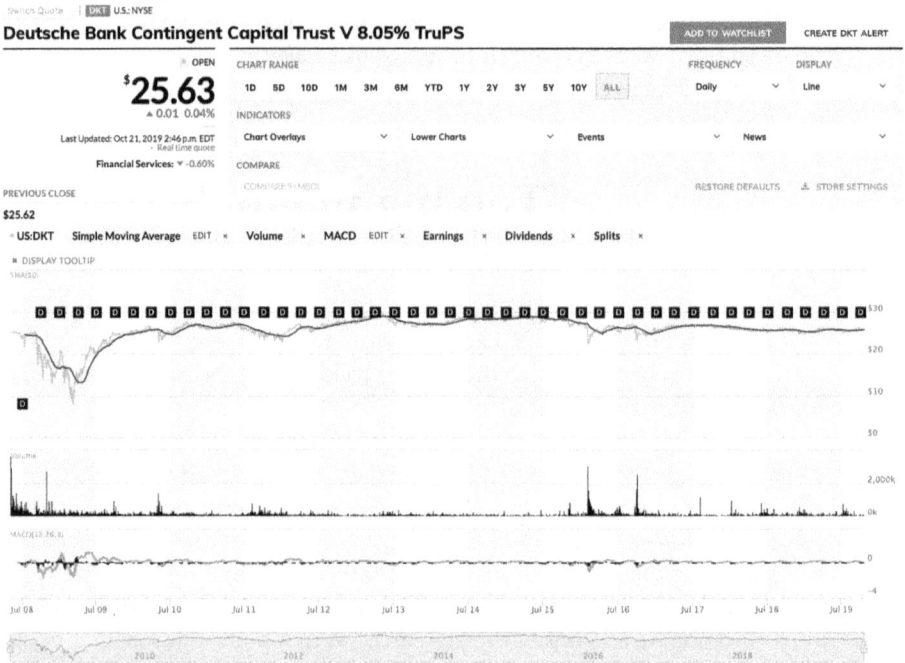

Figure 10

This is why preferred investors love a crash or temporary drop in the stock market. The opportunity to grab incredible yield and future capital gains.

Last thing to realize. Look at the DKT chart above. Notice how short the period was in which the stock steeply declined and how quickly it recovered. It was just a matter of months before the security regained almost full price again at $25 par. This is a commonality amongst all quality preferred shares: the way they recover after some kind of terrible event.

But why?

Two reasons.

During the slide, investors sell off for many reasons. Most need cash or they don't want to go down with the stock. But the most common reason… Margin.

Shares sold off from margin calls or other things, force an investor to sell whatever needs to be sold to cover that margin call. During these events investors unknowingly throw the baby out with the bath water. All this pressure, plus a thin trading market, causes the preferred shares to quickly plunge.

So why don't the shares stay down you might ask?

The quick answer is – the dividend. Investors go in to buy the attached value. As these shares slide to ridiculously low levels, the dividend yield grows almost exponentially. As the selling subsides smart investors will buy up those shares as long as they feel the issuing company is strong enough to survive. Before you know it, all the shares dumped during the sell-off are in demand because of the oversized yield which causes the share to rise to more reasonable levels. Once a reasonable point is reached the shares level off.

Marvin's story illustrates the magical returns possible with preferred stock. While financial meltdowns are uncommon, they still occur roughly once a decade. See below. Each drop is eventually followed by recovery. The only difference is that preferred often recover first and fastest because of the oversized yield created during the dislocation.

What that means to you is at least once a decade comes an unbelievable opportunity to invest in deeply discounted preferred shares.

When the time comes don't take it lightly, ACT.

Take your time, research, and invest in the best!

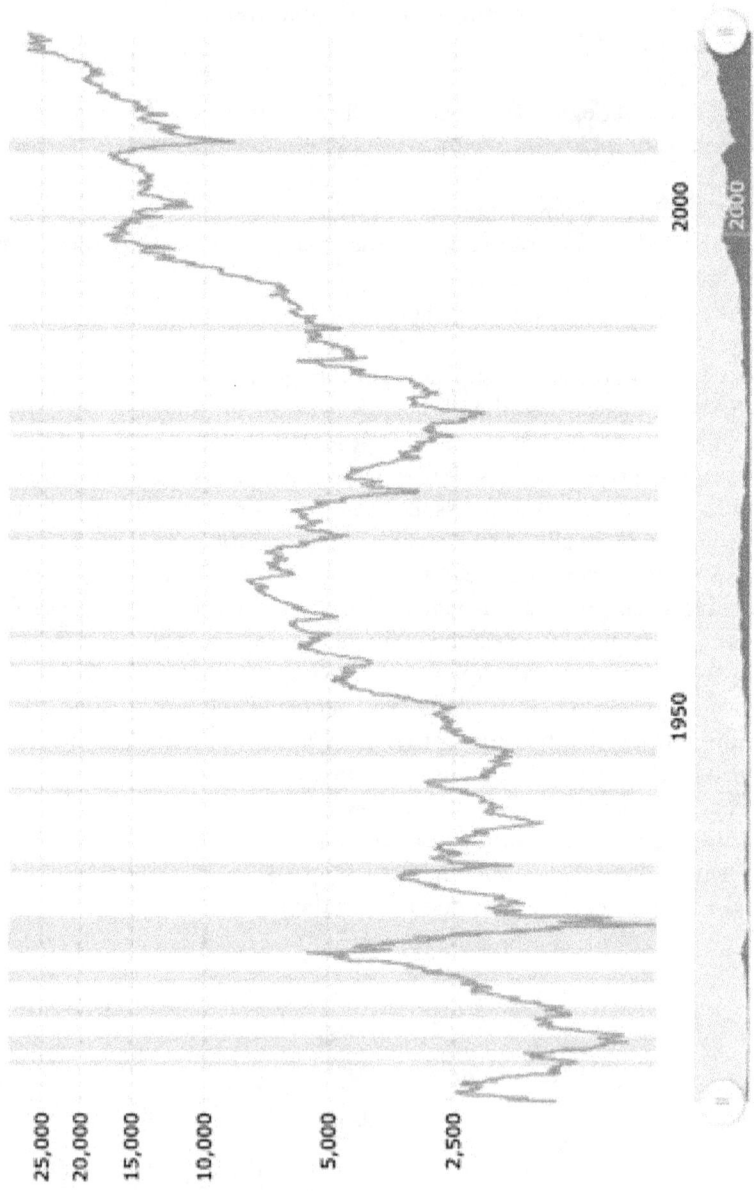

Figure 11

15

THEY PAY MORE

A T THIS POINT, I can imagine that you can see why preferred shares are worth the investment, but I also can imagine that one thing is still confusing: **why do preferred shares pay more than most other fixed income products**? Surprisingly, the answer has nothing to do with preferred stock itself as a security, but more how preferred stock is marketed to be sold.

If I was to ask you a question as to who do you believe chooses the dividend rate to be paid on a new preferred stock: the company issuing the preferred stock, or the underwriter taking it public? Who would you guess?

The logical assumption would be the issuer, being as it is their company and they would choose what dividend rate to pay, but oddly that would be incorrect.

Amazingly, it's not the preferred stock issuing company that determines the dividend to be paid on a new issue, instead it's actually the underwriters and their investment bankers who ultimately decide the dividend rate. Sounds crazy right? But it's true. The underwriter determines what dividend rate the issue will pay. Why? Several reasons.

First let's look at how a traditional **public stock offering** is sold from an issuer.

In this scenario the issuer, or its owners, sell a portion of the company's stock to public investors. This is usually done through an underwriting process where the company negotiates a sale of its stock to one or more investment banks that then act as underwriters and a syndicate group for the offering. The underwriters then each sell their stock to a much larger group of investors on **the public market**. With a common stock underwriting, the underwriters are compensated both through fees and the discounted stock they purchased from the issuer.

The risk in this involves whether or not the underwriter will be able to sell the stock they simultaneously buy from the issuer (that was discounted) for more than they paid for it.

So, the underwriters buy the shares selling them simultaneously. Here, the underwriters *could* face losses if the stock is sold for less than they paid. This *is* risky but, compared to a preferred stock offering, *the risk is small*.

In a **preferred stock offering**, things are very, *very* risky. Unlike a common stock offering where shares are simultaneously bought and then sold, with a preferred offering the preferred shares are often first bought by the underwriter from the issuer. The underwriter then puts up all the cash. **This is a direct purchase from the issuer** and is usually a tremendous amount of money – tens, hundreds of millions, and even billions of dollars. This purchase using the underwriter's cash, puts the underwriter at great risk.

To reduce the risk and recoup cash as fast as possible, the underwriter attempts to immediately unload those shares to "dealers" after purchase who in turn unload them to institutions, funds and individuals as quickly as possible. Because all these groups need assurances that the shares are marketable enough to be sold, the underwriter must figure out a dividend rate high enough, so they do not get left with any shares purchased from the issuing company and the dealers subsequently don't get stuck buying those shares from the underwriter.

In other words, **everyone in the chain need assurances that the dividend rate is high enough to make sure everyone can offload their shares.** Because of this concern, preferred dividend rates are not determined until a time right before the shares are finally offered. Maybe it's the right before maybe it's minutes before.

To make sure this happens a dividend rate higher than normal needs to be paid so as to incentivize all parties to complete the transaction. This results in a higher dividend rate paid on preferred stock.

Once agreed by the issuer and the underwriter, the declared dividend rate is added to the prospectus which is finalized and then filed with the SEC.

A term sheet is then distributed to the dealers.

After the prospectus is filed by the SEC, the issuer seeks regulatory approval and submits a trading application to an exchange such as the *New York Stock Exchange*.

Now the scary part…

The shares cannot begin to trade on the NYSE until the Exchange approves the application. No one knows exactly how long this takes. Maybe it will take three days, maybe it will take three weeks. This is absolutely terrifying to the underwriter who is bearing all the risk and is out the cash.

To avoid this waiting period and risk, underwriters came up with **a solution**. What underwriters do is they temporarily use the loosely-regulated Over-The-Counter (OTC) as a temporary bridge to sell those shares. Doing so greatly reduces the underwriters' risk allowing them to offload shares. The shares are then sold "wholesale" through the Over-The-Counter market under a temporary trading symbol.

How Does It Work?

How it works is that the underwriters usually buy shares in the newly created preferred stock for around $24.25 per share. As you may remember the underwriters, have used their own cash to buy the shares and want to sell these new shares quickly to its brokers and dealers, using the OTC exchange. That's when the temporary OTC **trading symbol is set up**.

The underwriter now can sell the shares to the brokers and dealers, marking them up $0.25 to $0.50 per share so they are now being sold somewhere in the range of $24.50 to $24.75 per share.

Now in the hands of the brokers and dealers, the brokers and dealers rush to offload those shares. During this wholesale window in time on the OTC, investors using online trading accounts can buy alongside institutions, purchasing shares often for less than the $25 offering price per share. Usually it is between $24.75 to $24.95 a share and this purchase of shares under the offering prospectus prices is called **purchasing wholesale**.

When the trading application to the NYSE is finally accepted then the shares migrate over and the stock symbol is changed one last time for good.

Once approval is given, this is considered the actual **Initial Public Offering** or **IPO date**.

One downside here is that brokerage firms and online brokers can run into problems trying to follow the change from a temporary trading symbol to a permanent one. *Note also some online platforms will not allow you to buy new preferred shares directly online, requiring instead a call-in to make a trade.*

On the other hand, some online brokerages can execute a trade online using the temporary OTC symbol.

Adding to the confusion, once a permanent stock symbol is given it may vary across different trading platforms. For reasons unknown, different online brokerages and quote services differ on how you reach a preferred stock symbol.

It is just the way it is.

Often, you will have to enter the name of the preferred stock to see how they are listing the symbol or even contact your online broker by phone or chat to see how they list that preferred stock. Once the preferred shares make the move from the OTC to the final exchange, such as the NYSE, they will be displayed in the way that individual brokerage firms and news outlets choose. Let's look at how preferred shares are displayed on different online news platforms and brokerage sites

Preferred Stock Symbols across Different Online Brokerage Sites and Platforms

As mentioned all online brokerage firms and platforms display preferred stocks symbols differently. Meaning that if you are looking up or trying to purchase or sell shares of preferred stock on one online brokerage firm and then switch to another online brokerage firm, the stock symbols will not be the same.

I wish I could explain why they chose to do it this way, but I cannot. Regardless, understand that each online trading platform and news site will list preferred share symbols differently. Below is a list of how each of the **larger sites** and **online broker houses** display preferred stock symbols, with examples based on the preferred stock of **New Residential Preferred A Shares**.

Brokerage Firm	Suffix	Example
ALLY	/PR	NRZ/PRA
E*Trade	.PR.	NRZ.PR.A
Fidelity	/P and PR	NRZ/PA or NRZPRA
Interactive Brokers	<SPACE>PR	NRZ PRA
Schwab	/PR	NRZ/PRA
Scottrade	p and P	NRZpA of NRZPA
T Rowe Price	<SPACE> PR	NRZ PRA
TD Ameritrade	<DASH>	NRZ-A

Online Websites		
Google Finance	<DASH>	NRZ-A
MarketWatch	.PR and .P	NRZ.PRA and PSA.PA
Morningstar	PR	NRZPRA
NYSE	PR	NRZPRA
Seeking Alpha	.P	NRZ.PA
Yahoo Finance	-P	NRZ-PA

Ready for More Tricks?

I've shared with you Marvin's "billionaire's secrets"; there now follow more chapters on how to refine your investor skills...

16

CREDIT RATING SERVICES

"I am concerned about the return of my money, then the
return on my money."
– Mark Twain

HY DO WE NEED credit rating services?
As we all want to see our money returned, credit rating services
are the first line of defense when considering a preferred stock
investment.

Just a quick scan of a company's credit rating can usually eliminate a potential preferred candidate for investment. Below is a quick explanation of credit ratings, the companies providing ratings and their use in capital markets.

One thing to remember is that credit ratings speak to "the perceived" credit quality of an individual debt issue and its possibility of default. **They are also a view of the past, and not of the future.** Since future events and developments cannot be foreseen, the assignment of credit ratings is not exact. More importantly, credit ratings are not absolute when it comes to a measure of default probability as they are *not guaranteed*. If you ever want a reminder of this fact look no further than the company *Enron*.

For those of you not familiar, *Enron Corporation* was an American energy and services company based in Houston, Texas. Founded in 1985, *Enron* employed approximately 29,000 people and was a major electricity, gas, communications and paper company, with claimed revenues of nearly $101 billion during 2000. *Fortune* had *Enron* as fifth on its *Fortune 500* list and even named it "America's Most Innovative Company" for six consecutive years.

At the end of 2001, it was revealed that *Enron*'s reported financial condition was created from sustained accounting fraud. The scandal also caused the dissolution of *Arthur Anderson* one of the world's largest accounting firms. *Enron* filed for bankruptcy on December 3, 2001.

So how was *Enron* rated? Did the credit agencies get it right? No!

Enron was actually rated INVESTMENT GRADE by all three credit agencies *Moody's, Standard and Poor's, and Fitch* **up, right up** until four days before it declared bankruptcy. None saw it coming until it was too late.

Keep that in mind when you are relying on the credit ratings.

Credit Ratings Value – Reasonable Understanding of a Company's Finances

"Know what you own and know why you own it."
- Peter Lynch

Credit rating services are valuable tools when investing, but always remember that the credit rating service's view is merely an educated guess. Credit ratings are not guarantees of credit quality or that a particular issuer or debt issue will pay.

There is a place for credit rating services as they do more due diligence on individual companies than individual analysts or research groups. As such they also have a 'reasonable' understanding of the company's financial situation.

Regardless do your homework before making a decision. Once you've made a decision, make sure to **re-evaluate your portfolio regularly**. As a wise holding today may not be a wise holding in the future.

The Main Three Credit Rating Agencies

Many credit rating agencies exist but the three services that most *Fortune 500* companies use to rate their preferred securities are:

- Standard and Poor's
- Moody's
- Fitch

STANDARD
&POOR'S

Standard and Poor's[7] began in 1860, when Henry Varnum first published Poor's *Of History of Railroads and Canals in the United States*. The book compiled comprehensive information about the financial and operational state of U.S. railroad companies.

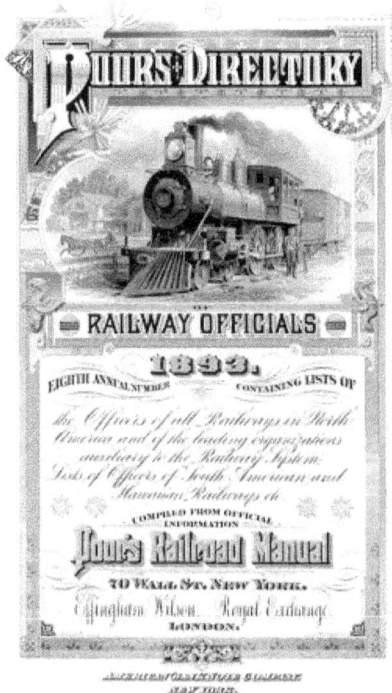

Separately, in 1906, Luther Lee began a company called the *Standard Statistics Bureau*, providing financial information on non-railroad companies.

The company became *Standard and Poor's* when in 1941, Paul Talbot Babson purchased *Poor's Publishing* and then merged it with *Standard Statistics*

---

[7] www.standardandpoors.com

to become *Standard & Poor's* nicknamed **S&P**. In 1966, *S&P* was bought by *McGraw-Hill* to get into the field of financial information services.

Today *S&P Global Ratings*, with its 10,000 employees, is the world's leading provider of credit ratings on more than 1 million government, corporate, financial entities and securities. Based in New York and in 28 countries worldwide, *S&P's* 1,500 analysts, managers and economists assess factors and trends that affect creditworthiness on over $46 trillion in debt. In 2016 alone, *S&P* rated more than $3.7 trillion in new debt and of all corporate sector investment-grade ratings issued, just 1% has defaulted over the most recent five-year period.

MOODY'S
INVESTORS SERVICE

Founded in 1900, *John Moody and Company* was the first manual providing basic statistics on stocks and bonds and is credited with being the inventor of modern bond ratings. The publication provided detailed statistics relating to stocks and bonds of financial institutions, government agencies, manufacturing, mining utilities and food companies. On its first print run the publication was an immediate success selling out in just two months.

From 1903 until the stock market crash of 1907 Moody's *Manual of Industrial and Miscellaneous Securities* was a national publication. In 1909 it was renamed Moody's investment service and was incorporated in 1914. In 1962, Moody's was acquired by Dunn and Bradstreet. It was later spun off becoming its own public company Moody's Investor Service in 2007.

Today *Moody's* is a leading provider of credit ratings and risk analysis, tracking debt covering more than 135 nations, 5,000 non-financial corporate issuers, 4,000

financial institutions, 18,000 public finance issuers and 11,000 structured finance transactions.

Moody's reported revenue of $4.2 billion in 2017, when it was employing 12,000 people across 42 countries.

The Scales

Moody's has the easiest ratings scale to understand as its ratings go from a simple Aaa down to a D. **Bbb** is the lowest to be considered **investment grade**. We have also included the *Fitch* rating system.

Moody's Rating System

Investment Grade

- **Aaa**: An obligor rated 'Aaa' has extremely strong capacity to meet its financial commitments. 'Aaa' is the highest issuer credit rating assigned by Standard & Poor's.
- **Aa**: An obligor rated 'Aa' has very strong capacity to meet its financial commitments. It differs from the highest-rated obligors only to a small degree. Includes:
- **A**: An obligor rated 'A' has strong capacity to meet its financial commitments but is somewhat more susceptible to the adverse effects of changes in circumstances and economic conditions than obligors in higher-rated categories.
- **Bbb**: An obligor rated 'Bbb' has adequate capacity to meet its financial commitments. However, adverse economic conditions or changing circumstances are more likely to lead to a weakened capacity of the obligor to meet its financial commitments.

Speculative Grade

- **Bb**: An obligor rated 'Bb' is less vulnerable in the near term than other lower-rated obligors. However, it faces major ongoing uncertainties and exposure to adverse business, financial, or economic conditions, which could lead to the obligor's inadequate capacity to meet its financial commitments.
- **B**: An obligor rated 'B' is more vulnerable than the obligors rated 'Bb', but the obligor currently has the capacity to meet its financial

commitments. Adverse business, financial, or economic conditions will likely impair the obligor's capacity or willingness to meet its financial commitments.

- **Ccc**: An obligor rated 'Ccc' is currently vulnerable, and is dependent upon favorable business, financial, and economic conditions to meet its financial commitments.
- **Cc**: An obligor rated 'Cc' is currently highly vulnerable.
- **C**: highly vulnerable, perhaps in bankruptcy or in arrears but still continuing to pay out on obligations
- **R**: An obligor rated 'R' is under regulatory supervision owing to its financial condition. During the pendency of the regulatory supervision, the regulators may have the power to favor one class of obligations over others or pay some obligations and not others.
- **SD**: has selectively defaulted on some obligations
- **D**: has defaulted on obligations and S&P believes that it will generally default on most or all obligations
- **NR**: not rated

Moody's Investors Service (www.moodys.com)

Numerical Modifiers

Within each rating between Aa and Caa, Moody's further subdivides bonds with numerical modifiers 1, 2 and 3 that indicate where a bond ranks within its rating category, with 1 being the best.

A rating of "Aa1," for example, means that the security is amongst the highest-quality in the "Aa" category, just a cut below the top-quality "Aaa" securities.

A rating of "Aa3," on the other hand, means the security is at the lower end of the "Aa" pool, close to "A" status. "Aaa" ratings don't have modifiers, nor do those below "Caa."

Fitch
Ratings

Fitch Rating System

Fitch ratings is an international credit rating agency out of New York City and London. Fitch bases the ratings on factors such as what kind of debt a company holds and how sensitive it is to systemic changes like interest rates. The Fitch rating system is very similar to Moody's in that they too use a letter system.

The Fitch rating system (which is the same as S&P) is as follows:

- AAA: companies of exceptionally high quality (established, with consistent cash flows)
- AA: still high quality; slightly more risk than AAA
- A: low default risk; slightly more vulnerable to business or economic factors
- BBB: low expectation of default; business or economic factors could adversely affect the company
- Non-investment grade
- BB: elevated vulnerability to default risk, more susceptible to adverse shifts in business or economic conditions; still financially flexibility
- B: degrading financial situation; highly speculative
- CCC: real possibility of default
- CC: default is a strong probability
- C: default or default-like process has begun
- RD: issuer has defaulted on a payment
- D: defaulted

Comparison Chart Moody – S&P – Fitch

Moody's	S&P	Fitch	Credit Worthiness
Aaa	AAA	AAA	An obligor has EXTREMELY STRONG capacity to meet its financial commitments.
Aa1	AA+	AA+	An obligor has VERY STRONG capacity to meet its financial commitments. It differs from the highest-rated obligors only to a small degree.
Aa2	AA	AA	
Aa3	AA−	AA−	
A1	A+	A+	An obligor has STRONG capacity to meet its financial commitments but is somewhat more susceptible to the adverse effects of changes in circumstances and economic conditions than obligors in higher-rated categories.
A2	A	A	
A3	A−	A−	
Baa1	BBB+	BBB+	An obligor has ADEQUATE capacity to meet its financial commitments. However, adverse economic conditions or changing circumstances are more likely to lead to a weakened capacity of the obligor to meet its financial commitments.
Baa2	BBB	BBB	
Baa3	BBB−	BBB−	
Ba1	BB+	BB+	An obligor is LESS VULNERABLE in the near term than other lower-rated obligors. However, it faces major ongoing uncertainties and exposure to adverse business, financial, or economic conditions which could lead to the obligor's inadequate capacity to meet its financial commitments.
Ba2	BB	BB	
Ba3	BB−	BB−	

Moody's	S&P	Fitch	Credit Worthiness
B1	B+	B+	An obligor is MORE VULNERABLE than the obligors rated 'BB', but the obligor currently has the capacity to meet its financial commitments. Adverse business, financial, or economic conditions will likely impair the obligor's capacity or willingness to meet its financial commitments.
B2	B	B	
B3	B−	B−	
Caa	CCC	CCC	An obligor is CURRENTLY VULNERABLE, and is dependent upon favorable business, financial, and economic conditions to meet its financial commitments.
Ca	CC	CC	An obligor is CURRENTLY HIGHY-VULNERABLE.
	C	C	The obligor is CURRENTLY HIGHLY-VULNERABLE to nonpayment. May be used where a bankruptcy petition has been filed.
C	D	D	An obligor has failed to pay one or more of its financial obligations (rated or unrated) when it became due.
e, p	Pr	Expected	Preliminary ratings may be assigned to obligations pending receipt of final documentation and legal opinions. The final rating may differ from the preliminary rating.
WR			Rating withdrawn for reasons including - debt maturity, calls, puts, conversions, etc., or business reasons (e.g. change in the size of a debt issue), or the issuer defaults.

Moody's	S&P	Fitch	Credit Worthiness
Unsolicited	Unsolicited		This rating was initiated by the ratings agency and not requested by the issuer.
	SD	RD	This rating is assigned when the agency believes that the obligor has selectively defaulted on a specific issue or class of obligations, but it will continue to meet its payment obligations on other issues or classes of obligations in a timely manner.
NR	NR	NR	No rating has been requested, or there is insufficient information on which to base a rating.

Investment vs Speculative Grade

Preferred stock is considered investment grade or **IG** by S&P if its credit rating is BBB or higher by *S&P*, or Baa3 or higher by Moody's, the so-called "Big Three" of credit agencies.

The threshold between investment-grade and speculative-grade ratings has important market implications for issuers' borrowing costs.

What is a Credit Rating Downgrade?

A credit rating downgrade is a negative change in the rating of a stock or bond. The downgrade will typically accompany a credit rating analysis that concludes that the future prospects for the company reviewed have changed from the original recommendation. This change can come in the form of material changes to the company's operations or even its industry.

When a preferred is downgraded, it might move from an "A" rating to a "BBB" rating. While a rating downgrade in this scenario is not material, other downgrades are more important and can have severe effects on the price and prospects of a particular preferred. If a preferred stock is downgraded from

"BBB," or investment grade, to "BB," which would be below investment grade, the ramifications could be significant as any portfolios that have been mandated to hold only investment-grade debt will need to sell that security.

Often this type of wide selling drives down the price of that preferred. If you hear that there has been a downgrade to below investment grade, then it's often a sign to **sell quickly** because, as more investors learn of the downgrade, you can anticipate more selling.

Furthermore, with there being more than one credit agency, if you had to guess – what do you think will happen if one credit agency downgrades a preferred? The answer – expect the others to follow. Once the other two agencies downgrade you can expect the security to continue selling off.

Let's look at a recent downgrade on Ford by *Moody's* on September 9th, 2019.

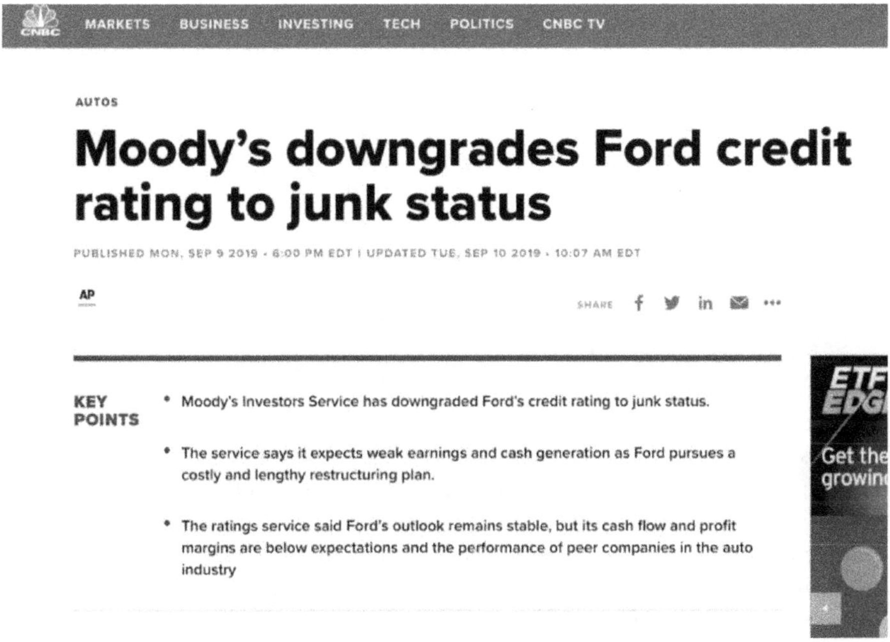
MARKETS BUSINESS INVESTING TECH POLITICS CNBC TV

AUTOS

Moody's downgrades Ford credit rating to junk status

PUBLISHED MON, SEP 9 2019 · 6:00 PM EDT | UPDATED TUE, SEP 10 2019 · 10:07 AM EDT

AP

SHARE

KEY POINTS

- Moody's Investors Service has downgraded Ford's credit rating to junk status.
- The service says it expects weak earnings and cash generation as Ford pursues a costly and lengthy restructuring plan.
- The ratings service said Ford's outlook remains stable, but its cash flow and profit margins are below expectations and the performance of peer companies in the auto industry

Figure 12

Fig. 13 shows how the stock reacted, dropping from $27.50 to $25.22 **immediately** following the downgrade:

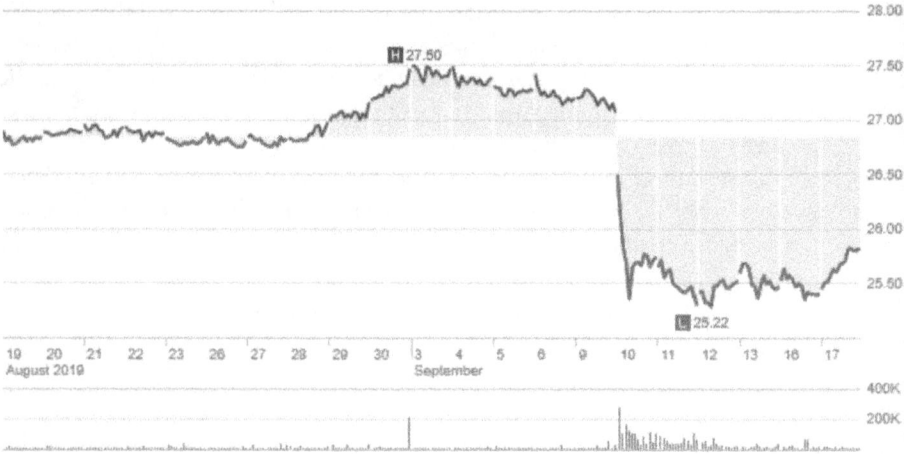

Figure 13

The Ford downgrade in this case was made by just one agency. Investors have not rushed back into the security as they wait for the other shoe (or shoes) to drop. The shoe in this case being either *S&P* or *Fitch*. Should the other two agencies lower their rating one would expect to see *Ford* preferred stock become weaker.

Downgrades are significant events and should not be ignored. The reasons for downgrades vary as most indicate problems such as an SEC investigation into a company's operations, or deteriorating fundamentals, or even because the marketplace no longer favors that particular company's business. If you hear the words **securities and exchange** in relation to the accounting procedures of your issuer, SELL IMMEDIATELY. Even if by doing so you incur a loss on the sale, you are making the right move, as SEC investigations into accounting rarely end without punishment. Even if an issuer was to resolve the issue with the SEC, it would take time and normally the security *will* suffer.

17

WHAT TO BUY?
SEVENS & THIRTEENS

BEFORE YOU PUT YOUR money into a preferred stock you need to ask: **CAN THE ISSUER PAY YOU BACK?**

If the answer is **NO**, run!

Hope is not a strategy.

If you were to ask Marvin for a loan, the first question he would ask is, "do you have good collateral"? Same goes for a preferred stock. That's the first thing you need to ask.

Here are the next seven things.

"The Quick Seven"

Before you buy any preferred stock, ask yourself these seven questions:

1. Is the issuer a large established company with assets?
2. Does the issuer have sufficient cash to pay the dividend and future dividends?

3. Does the issuer consistently pay its dividends without missing a payment?
4. Is the issuer profitable?
5. Are its cash flow and earnings great enough to payout dividends?
6. Are dividends cumulative so if they do miss payments, they have to make up that payment?
7. Will the company be able to keep paying dividends based on future earnings growth?

We know how preferred shares work.

We know to look at rating agencies.

But how do we know **what** to buy?

While investing is a personal preference there a few rules to keep in mind as we don't want to lose our money. These rules are meant to help you, the investor, make the best choice when investing in issues. This does not mean you cannot go outside the rules for one reason or another but remember – the further you move away from the rules, the more risk you're taking.

A problem with so many rules is that it feels as if there can be little to invest in despite there being 1,000 issues trading. But don't let that lead you astray! It's only your money!

Think of the rules as a tool to weed out the good from the bad. The rules apply for all preferred stocks regardless of industry.

Lastly, the goal here is to win, to collect the highest dividends possible and make capital gains; not to invest in as many preferred stocks as possible. Ten to thirty different preferred issuers are more than enough for most people's portfolios.

As with any investment, you want to separate the good eggs from the bad. To win and sleep at night you need to buy only the best. Now that you have narrowed down some preferred shares that you feel are good candidates, let's look at a more detailed list of criteria

Sure, we know low risk and profitable is a good start but here's another 13 points to buying the best, along with their reasons.

"13-Point Buying Plan"

1. **Buy American Companies**
    American companies follow American securities laws. Buying American greatly increases safety and reduces risk.
2. **Buy Profitable Companies Only**
    If a company is losing money how long until they suspend a

dividend? The answer, no one knows, but we do know that no company can lose money forever. To avoid this do not ever buy preferred stock in companies that are not profitable.

3. **Bigger is Better**

    How big is the company? *Fortune 500* companies are best. Buy companies with a minimum of $5 billion in market capitalization. Large profitable companies have a much better chance of paying than small companies.

4. **Buy a Strong Underwriter**

    Only buy preferred stock underwritten from the top ten underwriters. Think *Goldman Sachs, Morgan Stanley* types. If you have never heard of the underwriter taking the preferred stock public – stay away. There are plenty of quality issues being underwritten today so taking risks on small underwriters are just not necessary. Just think of it this way. Small underwriters just do not have the resources to find and finance the best candidates to take public. As such, often the product they bring to market is inferior which means more risk and *we do not like risk*. Further, small underwriters usually issue smaller, riskier, lesser known preferred securities that are less liquid.

5. **Buy Credit Rating**

    When buying a preferred stock, it must be a minimum investment grade of B according to the *Moody's, Standard and Poor's* or *Fitch* Rating Services. If it has no investment grade or a credit rating of C or lower, stay away. An easy way to remember is **B is buy and C is crap**. In reality look for a rating that is higher than a *Moody's* Ba3 or a *Standard and Poor's* BB. While credit rating agencies are not perfect, they do often give a better 'idea' as to a company's ability to repay its debts.

6. **Buy Dividend Rates over 6% Whenever Possible**

    Good quality issues paying dividends over 6% tend to trade strongly, compared to issues that pay lower rates. Also, those preferred with rates **over 6%** have a better chance of being redeemed by an issuer than those who trade **lower than 6%**. Most preferred stocks with rates under 5% are often not redeemed and are only redeemed in periods of abnormally low or zero rate environments. Typically, these less than 6% payers become 'yield traps' as the chance for these securities to be redeemed is small.

7. **Buy History and Track Record**

    Think, **"a leopard never changes its spots"**. Now ask, has the issuer ever suspended or not paid a dividend? If the answer is yes, pass on that issue. As goes the old expression, **"Fool me once shame on you, fool me twice shame on me."** If the company does not have a good track record, why take risk? It's only your money!

8. **Buy Cumulative Dividends**

Things happen but as a preferred stock buyer we want to be paid when things don't go well. How do we protect ourselves? Buy cumulative preferred stock. Why? Because cumulative dividends are to be paid either at the due date or at a later date. If a company cannot pay a cumulative dividend when due, it is still responsible for paying it in the future and it must fulfill this obligation before it can award dividends to common shareholders. Cumulative dividends are intended to ensure investors a minimum return on their investment in the company. A company that issues cumulative preferred stock must also disclose any accumulated, unpaid dividends in its financial statements.

9. **Buy Dividends Paid Quarterly**

Quarterly dividends come with a perk: you're paid four times a year. That dividend schedule also influences how preferred shares trade giving you the investor more opportunities to buy and sell. At least four times during the year the market price of the preferred will tend to move higher as an ex-dividend date moves closer and investors try to pick off the dividend. Additionally, preferred shares often move lower after the pay date. These movements in the preferred stock give rise to the opportunity to buy and sell these shares. Often the **best price to purchase comes after the pay date** and the **highest price to sell occurs closer to the dividend date**.

10. **Buy Non-Convertible Preferred.**

A convertible preferred stock is a security that can be converted from a preferred stock into the same issuer's common stock at a conversion ratio specified in the issuer's prospectus. Basically, it lays out how many shares of the company's common stock you will receive upon conversion for each preferred share. Normally as the investor you call the timing of the conversion, except when it's a mandatory conversion whereby the issuing company forces the conversion. So why does this matter and why should convertible preferred be avoided? The first reason is uncertainty. The future cannot be predicted and as easy as this could be a great deal it could also be a horrible deal. Remember the conversion formula is fixed but the stock market is not. Market movements could determine a winner or loser. Next, if you are forced to convert you will have to take whatever they offer. Lastly, once you are converted into common stock, you are no longer a preferred holder and all preferred benefits, including that juicy dividend, are gone.

11. **Buy Preferred with Online Access to a Prospectus**

If you cannot access a company's prospectus online you might just want to pass on that issue. The fact is most old preferred issues do not have online access to an original prospectus because they have been around much longer than the SEC's online **EDGAR system**. The problem is that without access to this information, you are flying blind not knowing what you are investing in. Not having access to the original prospectus means exposing yourself to all types of hidden issues.

12. Buy Preferred Shares That Are Callable in Five Years

Most preferred stocks issued today give the issuing company the right to buy back the shares at their original issue price or par, five years from the issue date. This is known as the call date. The call date is public information. As the call date approaches and the preferred stock could be called, the preferred issue begins to move towards its original issue price or par. This movement is called preferred gravity. In essence as the call date approaches, the preferred shares move towards par as investors who hold them higher will often sell them off knowing the shares could be called. Having a five-year call date gives reasons for the preferred share price to come back to par over a ten-year call date, which often allows a preferred share price to drift as no immediate call date is even insight.

13. Buy Fixed Rate Not Variable Rate Preferred

In Las Vegas there are certain bets called **sucker bets**. A sucker bet is a wager in which the expected return does not reflect the odds of winning and is significantly lower. Variable rate preferred is a sucker bet. Let's see why. As we know, when you buy a fixed rate preferred stock you know what the interest rates will be for the life of the security. That's different than a variable rate preferred. Variable preferred shares initially pay a lower fixed dividend upfront for a period of time, typically three to five years, in return for a future option to convert to a **floating rate** that is pegged to some amount plus **LIBOR** (London Interbank Offered Rate) or another index. The concept is you are being sold on the idea that if rates move in the future the floating rate will also move up and you will go along for the ride. But it's not exactly as it seems and the variable preferred knife cuts both ways.

On the face of it, the variable rate preferred stocks may seem like a good deal but, when you look more closely, you will discover that variable rate preferred is more of a gimmick and should be avoided.

Why?

Because, first, there is no way to know the probable return on your investment.

Secondly, variable rate preferred may not deliver as a security with an increasing dividend rate.

Why you might ask?

One word, redemption!

As soon as the variable preferred can convert to floating it usually has the ability to be redeemed. This is no accident. The dealer is dealing from the bottom of the deck and as such makes the bet a sucker bet by having the ability to pull the rug out from underneath, robbing you the investor of the better return you were sold on in the first place. So, if it looks to the issuer like the dividend rate will increase alongside rising interest rates, the issuer will call back the floating preferred and issue a new fixed preferred to replace it. It's that simple. The issuing company does not want to be on the hook for rising interest payments tied to the variable preferred. Hence why it's a gimmick.

Insidious, right? Now for the **real** kick in the pants…

Before, we spoke about rising interest rates; but **what happens if interest rates go lower?** It all sounded great before talk of lower interest rates. Now with interest rates going lower, the variable rate dividend will go lower too. So not only have you taken a lower introductory dividend rate for three to five years for an option of potential higher rates on conversion but now the variable rate will be lower too.

To add insult to injury, what do you think will happen to the price of your variable preferred stock as rates go lower? That's right it will go lower as well.

So with variable, not only did you sacrifice interest for the initial period, and not only are you getting less of a dividend after conversion, but you also may get to lose all you gained in dividends as the share price of the preferred moves much lower with little chance of it ever being called.

Think of it… the shares you bought at $25 may now be $18 or lower and you could be trapped with a low dividend and little chance of a call to bail you out.

18

COMMON METRICS

A S AN INCOME INVESTOR, all you should care about is whether the issuing company can pay you future dividends. Basically, you need to know – **does the preferred stock company make money or do they lose money?** That's it. Remember *we do not like risk or risky bets.* We only want to own preferred stocks that will be able to pay us dividends.

While the dates of preferred stock payments are known in advance for years to come, quarter-by-quarter or bi-annually, we must take additional steps to make sure they can pay, which essentially comes down to how the company manages its own cash flow.

That comes down to metrics.

Don't worry if you do not understand cash flow yet, we are going to simplify that in a moment.

Here are basic examples of the common metrics that you need to know:

Net Income:

Let's start with the easiest one – net income. Simply, if total revenues or sales are greater than total expenses, then the company has a profit and that profit is its net income. **Net income = profitable.** If the company has a net income – *it is profitable.*

Net Loss:

Conversely, if the company is losing money, it is operating at a **net loss**. The company is not profitable! Net loss is often referred to as a 'net operating loss' (NOL). A net operating loss occurs when all expenses exceed all the income or total revenue produced for a given period of time. Or a net loss is the amount of money the company lost after all the expenses had been paid during the period.

Free Cash Flow:

To understand free cash flow, all we need to do is look for how much cash the company has left over after paying all its bills. That's what free cash flow is. This is one of the most important metrics to understand. See **Statement of Cash Flows.**

Operating Cash Flow:

Similar to free cash flow, operating cash flow shows you if the company's operations produce a net positive amount of cash. Think of it as cash received from customers, less cash paid out to suppliers, to generate a net positive amount of cash.

Current Ratio:

Are the company's assets greater than its liabilities? Simply put – can the company sell its assets today if needed to meet **all** its liabilities? If not, there could be a problem.

Just like if you personally had more bills owed than you had assets that you could sell off plus cash in the bank in total. If you had no assets left, you couldn't pay dividends either.

This common metric speaks to a company's overall health. If the company has less in assets than its liabilities it may be over-leveraged and may be unable to secure loans.

Question: would you want to loan a company like this money knowing that even if they sold all their assets, they still could not pay you back? Well, if you buy a preferred stock in a company like this that's exactly what you are doing.

If current liabilities exceed current assets, the current ratio will be less than 1. **A current ratio of less than 1 indicates that the company may have problems meeting its short-term obligations.**

The higher the current ratio, the better shape the business is in and the more likely it is to weather storms. Know that a current ratio of 1 means you have just enough assets to meet your liabilities. You've broken even. You won't have any spare cash left over, but you won't end up in awful debt. Anything less than 1 spells potential trouble.

Quick Ratio:

Similar to current ratio, the quick ratio only looks at the amount of cash on hand and assets that can be quickly converted to cash (like accounts receivable). If the ratio is less than 1 it means the company most likely will not be able to pay its bills.

19
JUST SAY NO!

ONCE YOUR STOCKBROKER NOTICES your interest in preferred shares, he or she may suggest buying a **Preferred ETF** or **Exchange Traded Fund**. While the idea of an ETF, which is similar to a mutual fund holding many different preferred stocks of which you get a fractional piece for each, seems like a convenient way to invest in the preferred arena, just say no! ETF's were invented to provide a seemingly easy way for investors invest in a sector. Most preferred ETF's have a totally different objective than you do, and this includes safety.

Some preferred ETF's target a sector, while others target returns. Other than convenience, preferred ETF's do not meet the criteria of what you as a preferred investor are looking for and contain much greater risk.

ETF's make money from fees. To attract investors preferred ETF's at times can show superior returns. To achieve these returns ETF's often spike the punch, buying speculative preferred shares, earning extraordinarily high dividends that come with substantial exposure to risk and default.

Why would the fund manager do this?

One word – greed.

The higher dividends can provide strong returns over the short run, attracting gullible investors to the fund and raising his or her pay. All this exposure to risky preferred shares may pay off during the short run but over time and in weaker markets, fund managers get hit with defaults, dividend suspensions and other things. As risk averse investors who do not like risk, we do not like ETF's either.

20

DIFFERENT TAXES

I PERSONALLY NEVER LET a tax decision guide my investments or the opportunity to take a profit on a stock. With preferred shares there are two distinctions which will decide your tax rate. The tax characteristics of preferred securities can vary and can be attractive to both the issuer and the investor.

To understand the tax treatment of income you receive from preferred securities know that it comes down to one question – Has the company paid its tax or not on the dividends they will use to pay you?

Qualified & Non-Qualified Dividends

The IRS recognizes two major categories of dividends:

* qualified
* non-qualified

The differences between the two lie in the way you pay taxes on each of them.

Qualified Dividends (QDI)

Qualified dividends (QDI) are taxed at the same rate as long-term capital gains, or 20 percent, or less. Companies who pay preferred stock dividends out of after-tax profits, who are taxed at the special 20 percent tax rate are referred to as "Qualified Dividend Income" or QDI. QDI preferred stocks are often seen as favorable for holding in a non-retirement account. To qualify for the qualified dividend rate, the dividend must also be paid by a corporation in the United States or with specific ties to the USA.

Holding Period for Qualified Dividends

To receive preferential tax treatment as qualified dividends, shares must be held, per IRS requirements, for at least 61 days during the 121-day period that begins 60 days before a company declares its dividends.

Non-Qualified Dividends

Investors are required to pay taxes on income earned from non-qualified dividends at the same rates that they are taxed on ordinary income, such as salary or wages from work.

The tax rates for ordinary income, including non-qualified dividends, have ranged from 10% to 39.6% since 2016.

The income breakdown for these rates is as follows:

> 10%: Single filers earning less than $9,275 and married filers earning less than $18,550.
> 15%: Single filers earning from $9,275 to $37,650 and married filers earning from $18,550 to $75,300.
> 25%: Single filers earning from $37,650 to $91,150 and married filers earning from $75,300 to $151,900.
> 28%: Single filers earning from $91,150 to $190,150 and married filers earning from $151,900 to $231,450.
> 33%: Single filers earning from $190,150 to $413,350 and married filers earning from $231,450 to $413,350.
> 35%: Single filers earning from $413,350 to $415,050 and married filers earning from $413,350 to $466,950.
> 39.6%: Single filers earning more than $415,050 and married filers earning more than $466,950.

REITs Tax Treatment

REITs are not QDI investments. REITs or 'real estate investment trusts', are companies that own or finance income-producing real estate. REITs are required to distribute at least 90 percent of their pre-tax profits to shareholders. Distributing this pre-tax profit is typically done as preferred stock dividends and because these dividend payments consist of 'pre-tax' dollars, dividends received from REITs are taxed as regular income and do not qualify for the special dividend tax rate. The same is true for dividends received from partnerships, since each partner is responsible for their own tax obligations.

21

SEC'S EDGAR SYSTEM

ALL COMPANIES ISSUING SECURITIES in the United States file with the SEC. The documents they file provide information to investors. The SEC allows anyone to access its database of files anytime through the internet. To review any company filing, you need to go to the SEC website www.sec.gov. Once there, you can go to the top right corner and click *company filings*. From there you will be led to another page where you can enter the name of the issuing company to locate information.

To narrow down all the filings look for **FWP** (Free Writing Prospectus), which appears like a term sheet, or **SEC form number 424(b)**. When you see either FWP or 424(b) you will know that you have found the filing for new preferred shares that will be or have been issued. Click on the link and you can see the FWP and the final prospectus.

Below you can see a recent FWP and Final Prospectus for a Ford 6.2% Exchange Traded Debt Security EDTS (preferred stock's kissing cousin, remember!) The EDGAR system is not difficult to use – it just takes a little time to learn.

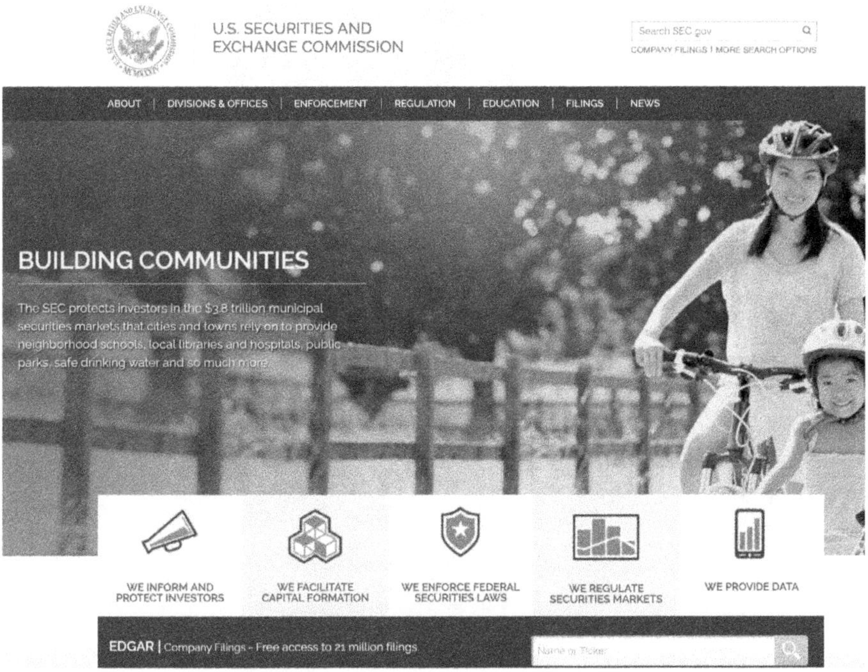

Figure 14

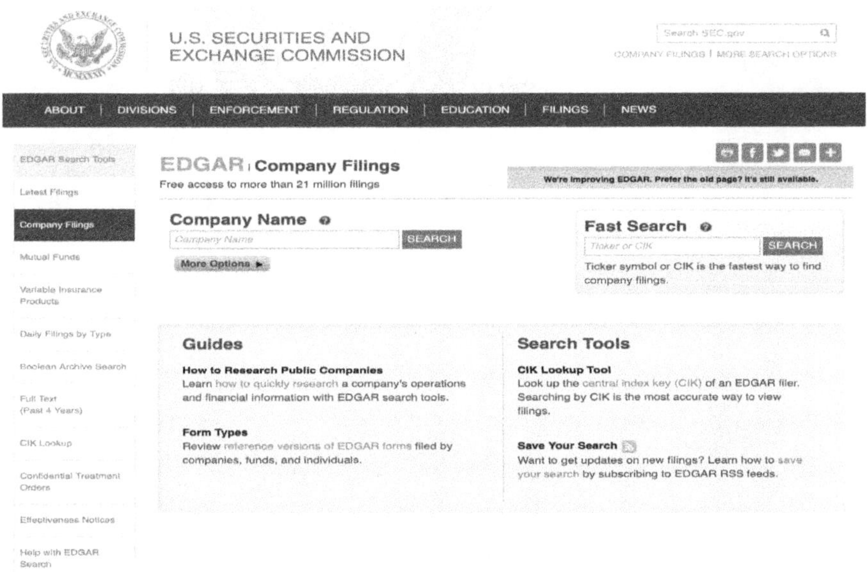

Figure 15

EDGAR Search Results

SEC Home ▸ Search the Next-Generation EDGAR System ▸ Company Search ▸ Current Page

FORD MOTOR CO CIK#: 0000037996 (see all company filings)

SIC: 3711 - MOTOR VEHICLES & PASSENGER CAR BODIES
State location: MI | State of Inc.: **DE** | Fiscal Year End: 1231
(Assistant Director Office: 5)
Get insider transactions for this **issuer.**
Get insider transactions for this **reporting owner.**

Business Address	Mailing Address
ONE AMERICAN ROAD	ONE AMERICAN RD
DEARBORN MI 48126	DEARBORN MI 48126
3133223000	

Filter Results:	Filing Type:	Prior to: (YYYYMMDD)	Ownership? ○ include ◉ exclude ○ only	Limit Results Per Page 40 Entries	Search Show All

Items 1 - 40 🔲 RSS Feed

Filings	Format	Description	Filing Date	File/Film Number
424B2	Documents	Prospectus [Rule 424(b)(2)] Acc-no: 0001047469-19-003235 (33 Act) Size: 272 KB	2019-05-21	333-216126 19843339
FWP	Documents	Filing under Securities Act Rules 163/433 of free writing prospectuses Acc-no: 0001104659-19-030529 (34 Act) Size: 29 KB	2019-05-20	333-216126 19838513
424B3	Documents	Prospectus [Rule 424(b)(3)] Acc-no: 0001047469-19-003200 (33 Act) Size: 269 KB	2019-05-20	333-216126 19837766
8-K	Documents	Current report, Item 5.07 Acc-no: 0000037996-19-000032 (34 Act) Size: 69 KB	2019-05-14	001-03950 19822129
S-8	Documents	Securities to be offered to employees in employee benefit plans Acc-no: 0001104659-19-023990 (33 Act) Size: 192 KB	2019-04-26	333-231058 19770670
8-K	Documents	Current report, Items 1.01, 2.03, and 9.01 Acc-no: 0001104659-19-023786 (34 Act) Size: 1 MB	2019-04-26	001-03950 19769035

Figure 16

FWP

Free Writing Prospectus
Filed Pursuant to Rule 433
Registration Number 333-216126

Ford Motor Company
Final Term Sheet

6.200% Notes due 2059

Issuer:	Ford Motor Company
Trade Date:	May 20, 2019
Settlement Date:	May 28, 2019 (T+5)
Stated Maturity:	June 1, 2059
Principal Amount:	$750,000,000
Interest Rate:	6.200%
Yield to Maturity:	6.200%
Price to Public:	100.000% of principal amount plus accrued interest from the Settlement Date
Underwriting Discount:	1.000% with respect to Notes sold to institutional investors 3.150% with respect to Notes sold to retail investors
Net Proceeds (Before Expenses) to Issuer:	$726,542,968.75
Interest Payment Dates:	Quarterly on each March 1, June 1, September 1, and December 1, beginning September 1, 2019 (long first coupon)
Redemption Provision:	The Notes may be redeemed, in whole or in part, on or after June 1, 2024, at a redemption price equal to 100% of the principal amount of the Notes to be redeemed, plus accrued and unpaid interest to the redemption date.
Over-Allotment Option:	None
Listing:	Ford intends to apply to list the Notes on the New York Stock Exchange
Joint Book-Running Managers:	BofA Securities, Inc. Morgan Stanley & Co. LLC RBC Capital Markets, LLC Wells Fargo Securities, LLC
Joint Lead Managers:	Citigroup Global Markets Inc. J.P. Morgan Securities LLC
Co-Managers:	Barclays Capital Inc. BMO Capital Markets, LLC Credit Suisse Securities (USA) LLC Goldman Sachs & Co. LLC
CUSIP/ISIN:	345370 845 / US3453708451

Figure 17

115

Final Prospectus

A final prospectus is the final version of a prospectus for a public offering of securities. This document is complete in all details concerning the offering and is referred to as a "statutory prospectus" or "offering circular." We also discussed these on page 37, but here is another example; this time from *Ford*.

Figure 18

22

MANAGING RISK

W HEN MANAGING RISK AS a preferred stock investor, I often think of the opening paragraph from the novel *A Tale of Two Cities*.

> *'It was the best of times, it was the worst of times, it was the age of wisdom, it was the age of foolishness, it was the epoch of belief, it was the epoch of incredulity, it was the season of light, it was the season of darkness, it was the spring of hope, it was the winter of despair. We had everything before us, we had nothing before us, we were all going direct to Heaven, we were all going direct the other way...'*
> **– Charles Dickens**

This phrase has great literary value in its use of comparison and contrast. Preferred shares are no different. Many possible outcomes, from two situations and environments. As a preferred stock investor our goal is to avoid investing in companies that could stop paying dividends or go bankrupt. Let's look at things we can do to protect ourselves and benefit from a changing market.

For years we have been in a period of low interest rates. As such, preferred holders have to be aware that when rates increase again the shares of preferred shares that were recently purchased will probably decrease as newer higher paying preferred become more desirable. That is not the end of the story. Decreasing preferred share prices can be a great buying opportunity as rates rarely go straight up or down.

Examples and Possible Outcomes

Let's pretend last month you bought a preferred share at $25 paying a dividend coupon of 6%. A few months later the federal reserve raises rates significantly. New preferred shares of similar quality are now being issued at $25 but pay 7%.

Which do you want to own?

Obviously, the 7% issue.

That same sentiment is shared by all investors who want more return.

But what happens to the $25, 6% preferred you already own?

That's right, it will go down as demand for the 6% preferred lessens and the demand for 7% preferred increases.

So, what should you do as an investor?

The answer depends the direction of interest rates. Understand this – rarely, if ever, do interest rate increases go up or down **in a straight line**. Yes, the federal reserve may lift rates a ¼ of a point or ½ a point from time-to-time, but it is less common for them to raise rates continually with regularity. Also, many other factors affect rates and because of these factors, rates increase or decrease **gradually**.

Because of this reality, periods of small increases in interest rates often present great buying opportunities of preferred shares at lower prices. While overall share prices may go lower temporarily, as a preferred investor we only care about the share price if we are selling.

For the time being these share price depressions are trivial in the sense that we will continue to receive dividends paid on each share we own regardless of the share's trading price. But as the price decreases an opportunity arises to buy more shares below par effectively raising our dividend yield as we now have a lower ownership price per share.

How to Profit from Changing Prices

Once again let's look at our $25 preferred that is paying us 6%. As mentioned in our example, newer preferred shares are now paying 7% coupons.

The 6% coupon preferred shares start decreasing in price as nervous sellers, fearful about the change in interest rates, sell the $25, 6% shares causing them to go down in price.

How low can they go?

Ask yourself at what price do you think these shares might fall to potentially, before they level off?

The answer is probably around $21.50 or when our 6% preferred then yields the same as the 7% preferred.

Why?

Because a $25 preferred share paying 6% has a dividend payment of $1.50 a year ($25 x 6%= $1.50.) If we take that yearly dividend payment $1.50 and divide it by $21.50, we can see that the new yield on shares purchased at $21.50 would now be 6.976% which we can round up to 7%. Once the dividend yield comes close to or equals 7% the shares will begin to attract buyers who can not only get the same effective yield but also have $3.50 of potential upside in capital gains if called.

This is the difference in buying preferred shares over common shares diverges. Essentially when share prices drop preferred investors buy more shares. This behavior is the polar opposite of how common share investors react. Common stock investors looking for income follow the market mantra - buy low, sell high. Because this is the strategy when the market goes down common shareholders sell in order to cut their losses.

Preferred shareholders conversely make their income from dividends. As we know dividends are paid based on the number of shares you own per share. Dividends amounts paid do not vary as the preferred stock price goes up or down as the dividend payment in most situations is constant. However, unlike common stock investors who sell when prices decline, preferred shareholders see opportunity to buy and accumulate more dividend-paying shares at sale or discount prices increasing their income and yield.

It is of paramount importance to understand how common stock and preferred share investing differ. **Preferred stock investors who follow the common stock investment strategy will fail** if investing in preferred shares.

While lower stock prices are something preferred share buyers relish, there are a few preferred traps along the way to avoid such as "The Forever Ownership Trap" and "The Yield Trap".

The Forever Ownership Trap

Who doesn't like a bargain? As we saw, buying preferred at lower share prices are sometimes a good way to boost yield but what happens when you purchase shares of a lower coupon that continue to drop in price?

Or worse, what if that preferred has dropped in price so much that it can't be sold without taking a loss and the issuer won't redeem or call those shares back?

Answer in these scenarios you have been caught in a "forever ownership trap". It's an insidious trap that plays on greed.

As we know, when preferred shares are called, you, the investor receive par value (usually $25 per share) back in cash in exchange for your shares from the issuer.

But what if that day never comes?

There is the problem. Or as Hamlet would say, "Ay, there's the rub!" Combine that with little or no interest from the public in buying those shares and you get to see the problem.

No buyer, few bids, can't sell.

In this scenario the only way out is to slowly average down your position over time, getting to a price that's even with the market and then hoping for a greater fool to take you out. This is a precarious position as hope is not a great strategy. If rates decline, others could look to buy you out of your position. If rates go higher though, you are stuck and the price of your preferred may even go lower. Yes, you will be collecting dividends quarterly as long as the company is doing fine but it will be difficult to ever get your cash out without the buyers.

To avoid this let's look to see what has happened in the past. Historically, preferred shares with a coupon of 6.5% or greater are almost always called by their issuer, with preferred stocks below 6.5% being less likely to be called. So, how can we avoid the forever ownership trap? Simply by avoiding purchasing low-dividend coupon shares, even when they look enticing.

Buy preferred as close to 6.5% as possible to keep clear of the forever ownership trap.

The Yield Trap

If you've heard the expression "if something sounds too good to be true then it probably is" then you get the basic concept of a yield trap. A yield trap is a stock with a dividend yield that's too good to be true because in the future it probably won't pay or even worse ir might go bankrupt. This also goes by the name "dividend yield trap" or "dividend trap."

Look, we'd all love a preferred stock that offers a double-digit yield, right? In reality though, outside great stress on the financial system, this opportunity just doesn't exist without taking on tremendous risk. In the preferred stock world, it can be tempting to look down a list of preferred stocks picking and choosing the ones with the highest yields. But doing this is often a serious mistake! You have to ask yourself, why is this stock paying *that much more*? Buying one of these may be buying into a yield trap meaning, ie. its dividend is not sustainable.

Here's how to spot and avoid dividend yield traps, and what you should look for instead.

Signs That a Stock Might Be a Dividend Yield Trap

There's no magic formula to detect a dividend yield trap but, here are some red flags:

- Unusually high yield: The most obvious sign is a dividend yield that is unusually high.
- Excessive debt: The more debt a company has, the more likely it is that it won't pay its dividend in tough times.
- Dividends greater than earnings: A company not earning enough profit to pay its dividend may be financing it through debt or other means.
- Little or negative cash flow: Cash flow is the difference between the money coming into a business and going out of the business. No cash flow? Then it's just a matter of time until no dividends either.
- Problems with the business: Is there something wrong with the business itself? If a high dividend yield is due to a decline in stock price, research why the stock's price dropped. Another indicator is declining earnings or growth.

An Example of a Dividend Yield Trap:

Fortress Biotech

Fortress Biotech, Inc. develops and commercializes pharmaceutical and biotechnology products. It markets dermatology products, such as *Targadox* for acne and *Exelderm* for ringworm and jock itch symptoms.

Fortress's stock has declined since issuance, never regaining its $25 par offering price.

Fortress Biotech, Inc. (FBIOP)

NasdaqGS - NasdaqGS Real Time Price. Currency in USD

☆ Add to watchlist   👥 Visitors trend 2W ↓ 10W ↑ 9M ↑

20.84 -0.05 (-0.24%)

At close: August 30 3:43PM EDT

Buy   Sell

Summary | Company Outlook (NEW) | Chart | Conversations | Statistics | Historical Data | Profile | Financials | Analysis | Options

Previous Close	20.89	Market Cap	111.866M	
Open	20.87	Beta (3Y Monthly)	2.46	
Bid	19.62 x 900	PE Ratio (TTM)	N/A	
Ask	22.53 x 1000	EPS (TTM)	-1.12	
Day's Range	20.80 - 20.90	Earnings Date	Nov 7, 2019 - Nov 11, 2019	
52 Week Range	11.90 - 21.95	Forward Dividend & Yield	N/A (N/A)	
Volume	6,724	Ex-Dividend Date	N/A	
Avg. Volume	5,310	1y Target Est	N/A	
Analyst Recommendation	N/A	Fair Value View details	N/A	

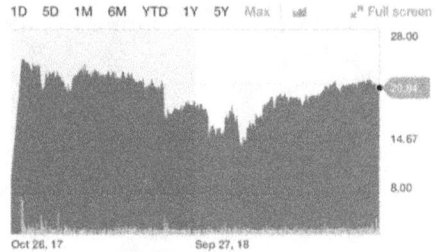

1D 5D 1M 6M YTD 1Y 5Y Max 📊   ⤢ Full screen

28.00 / 20.94 / 14.67 / 8.00

Oct 26, 17   Sep 27, 18

Trade prices are not sourced from all markets

View more ideas

All | 🔵 Short Term | 🔵 Mid Term | 🔵 Long Term

Figure 19 The common stock has declined from a high of $10 per share to roughly $2 per share.

Fortress Biotech, Inc. (FBIO)

NasdaqGS - NasdaqGS Real Time Price. Currency in USD

☆ Add to watchlist   👥 Visitors trend 2W ↑ 10W ↑ 9M ↑

1.8100 +0.0200 (+1.12%)

At close: August 30 4:00PM EDT

Buy   Sell

Summary | Company Outlook (NEW) | Chart | Conversations | Statistics | Historical Data | Profile | Financials | Analysis | Options

Previous Close	1.7900	Market Cap	122.872M	
Open	1.7900	Beta (3Y Monthly)	3.28	
Bid	1.7200 x 800	PE Ratio (TTM)	N/A	
Ask	1.8400 x 1800	EPS (TTM)	-1.1190	
Day's Range	1.7800 - 1.8400	Earnings Date	Aug 12, 2019 - Aug 16, 2019	
52 Week Range	0.4900 - 2.5900	Forward Dividend & Yield	N/A (N/A)	
Volume	256,612	Ex-Dividend Date	N/A	
Avg. Volume	424,453	1y Target Est	7.50	
Analyst Recommendation	N/A	Fair Value View details	Overvalued	

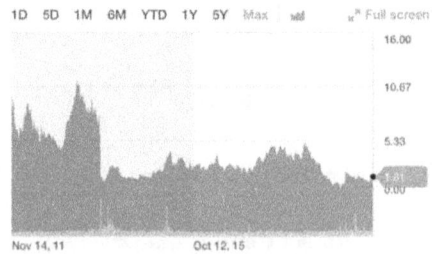

1D 5D 1M 6M YTD 1Y 5Y Max 📊   ⤢ Full screen

16.00 / 10.67 / 5.33 / 1.81 / 0.00

Nov 14, 11   Oct 12, 15

Trade prices are not sourced from all markets

View more ideas

All | 🔵 Short Term | 🔵 Mid Term | 🔵 Long Term

Figure 20 While gross profit has increased, operating loss and net loss has increased as well. They are losing money

Fortress Biotech, Inc. (FBIO)
NasdaqGS - NasdaqGS Real Time Price. Currency in USD

☆ Add to watchlist   ≋ Visitors trend 2W ↑ 1

1.8100 +0.0200 (+1.12%)
At close: August 30 4:00PM EDT

Buy   Sell

Summary   Company Outlook ⬤   Chart   Conversations   Statistics   Historical Data   Profile   **Financ**

5G Stocks Set To Soar
Learn about the 3 companies poised to dominate the sector for years. Breakthrough Investor

OPEN

Show: **Income Statement** | Balance Sheet | Cash Flow

Income Statement   All numbers in thousands

Annual | Quarterly

Revenue	12/31/2018	12/31/2017	12/31/2016	12/31/2015
Total Revenue	26,882	17,245	16,480	863
Cost of Revenue	6,125	3,658	11,495	-
Gross Profit	**20,757**	**13,587**	**4,985**	**863**
Operating Expenses				
Research Development	87,383	52,486	35,134	29,810
Selling General and Administrative	53,371	48,697	32,915	21,584
Non Recurring	-	-	-	-
Others	-	-	-	-
Total Operating Expenses	146,879	104,841	80,089	51,394
Operating Income or Loss	**-119,997**	**-87,596**	**-63,609**	**-50,531**
Income from Continuing Operations				
Total Other Income/Expenses Net	-10,803	-9,917	-7,681	-3,352
Earnings Before Interest and Taxes	-119,997	-87,596	-63,609	-50,531
Interest Expense	-10,340	-7,687	-3,691	-1,484
Income Before Tax	-130,800	-97,513	-71,290	-53,883
Income Tax Expense	-	1,513	-	-
Minority Interest	17,891	67,929	44,473	27,427
Net Income From Continuing Ops	**-130,800**	**-97,513**	**-71,290**	**-53,883**
Non-recurring Events				
Discontinued Operations	-11,136	-2,323	-2,323	-2,323
Extraordinary Items	-	-	-	-
Effect Of Accounting Changes	-	-	-	-
Other Items	-	-	-	-
Net Income				
Net Income	**-84,147**	**-66,876**	**-55,095**	**-48,428**
Preferred Stock And Other Adjustments	-	-	-	-
Net Income Applicable To Common Shares	**-84,147**	**-66,876**	**-55,095**	**-48,428**

Figure 21 Net loss is increasing every year.

Cash Flow <small>All numbers in thousands</small>

Period Ending	12/31/2018	12/31/2017	12/31/2016	12/31/2015
Net Income	-84,147	-66,876	-55,095	-48,428
Operating Activities, Cash Flows Provided By or Used In				
Depreciation	2,059	1,260	1,127	26
Adjustments To Net Income	-24,915	-14,973	4,718	22,522
Changes In Accounts Receivables	2,260	-5,928	-1,830	-1,830
Changes In Liabilities	4,663	10,823	5,395	5,889
Changes In Inventories	-507	32	-203	-203
Changes In Other Operating Activities	-680	-8,784	-1,390	-701
Total Cash Flow From Operating Activities	**-98,848**	**-81,305**	**-45,812**	**-20,378**
Investing Activities, Cash Flows Provided By or Used In				
Capital Expenditure	-7,082	-648	-6,370	-283
Investments	18,398	-36,002	-36,002	20,002
Other Cash flows from Investing Activities	9,782	-209	-6	-136
Total Cash Flows From Investing Activities	**18,824**	**-40,224**	**-6,060**	**7,885**
Financing Activities, Cash Flows Provided By or Used In				
Dividends Paid	-2,344	-299	-299	-299
Sale Purchase of Stock	-	-	-	-
Net Borrowings	17,299	37,161	6,137	10,000
Other Cash Flows from Financing Activities	28,067	88,301	36,145	50,641
Total Cash Flows From Financing Activities	**50,648**	**150,381**	**42,905**	**60,916**
Effect Of Exchange Rate Changes	-	-	-	-
Change In Cash and Cash Equivalents	**-29,376**	**28,852**	**-8,967**	**48,423**

Figure 22 Fortress does have cash, but it has declined to its lowest level in years.

Lastly, as you will see in fig.23 on the next page, its net assets are down heavily.

Fortress displays many of the characteristics of yield trap with its high yield, excessive debt, dividends greater than earnings, and a high dividend yield with a declining stock. Even more, the preferred shares have no credit rating.

What do you think? How long can they pay the dividend?

Who knows?

Maybe a week, a year… or forever?

What will cause the stock to go back to par? None of the answers are clear. For these reasons, the stock *appears to be a dividend trap.*

Balance Sheet All numbers in thousands

Period Ending	12/31/2018	12/31/2017	12/31/2016	12/31/2015
Current Assets				
Cash And Cash Equivalents	65,508	94,952	88,294	98,182
Short Term Investments	17,604	36,002	2,212	-
Net Receivables	7,593	8,376	8,689	156
Inventory	678	171	203	-
Other Current Assets	13,089	37,948	1,175	-
Total Current Assets	**111,207**	**183,181**	**109,634**	**99,937**
Long Term Investments	-	1,390	1,414	2,485
Property, plant and equipment	12,019	7,116	7,376	309
Goodwill	-	18,645	18,645	-
Intangible Assets	1,417	883	17,408	1,250
Accumulated Amortization	-	-	-	-
Other Assets	16,350	53,380	16,254	14,629
Deferred Long Term Asset Charges	-	-	-	-
Total Assets	**140,993**	**245,950**	**170,731**	**118,610**
Current Liabilities				
Accounts Payable	17,856	10,002	14,213	1,868
Short/Current Long Term Debt	19,078	13,228	2,031	-
Other Current Liabilities	1,291	32,651	21,796	4,984
Total Current Liabilities	**55,614**	**71,438**	**56,565**	**10,579**
Long Term Debt	60,425	49,271	26,184	23,174
Other Liabilities	5,211	4,739	5,014	584
Deferred Long Term Liability Charges	-	-	-	-
Minority Interest	17,891	67,929	44,473	27,427
Negative Goodwill	-	-	-	-
Total Liabilities	**121,250**	**125,448**	**87,763**	**34,337**
Stockholders' Equity				
Misc. Stocks Options Warrants	-	-	-	-
Redeemable Preferred Stock	-	-	-	-
Preferred Stock	-	-	-	-
Common Stock	58	51	49	47
Retained Earnings	-396,274	-312,127	-245,251	-190,156
Treasury Stock	659	500	-	-
Capital Surplus	397,408	364,148	283,697	246,955
Other Stockholder Equity	659	500	-	-
Total stockholders' equity	1,851	52,572	38,495	56,846
Net Tangible Assets	**434**	**51,689**	**2,442**	**55,596**

Figure 23

23

GRANDMA SHARES

AFTER A FEW CRASHES, many investors have had enough pulling out of the stock market for fear that a new crash will wreck their investments further. This is a sad reality amongst many investors I meet between the ages of 45-60. They got crushed and never went back.

The problem with this is that putting funds into CD's while they're safe goes back to what we discussed earlier in this book about how money becomes worth less over time and that if you are not gaining, you are essentially losing.

Had these investors chosen **grandma preferred** rather than a savings account or CD's they could have increased their return two, three, four, or five-fold; investing in super stable companies, mostly utilities with dividend payment histories going back before many were even born. Grandma shares are perfect for the mot fearful.

These shares, quietly hidden amongst the thousand or so preferred stocks listed, are a few dozen issues that have been trading for more than 80 years. Most are utility preferred and industrial types. Shares like *Alabama Power* or *Niagara Mohawk* or *Connecticut Light & Power Co.*, issued between 1930 and 1980 have come to be known as "grandma shares".

Why grandma shares?

Because they were bought and held decades ago for dividend income never to be sold, paying a lifetime of dividends to Grandma. Further, these shares paid dividends regardless of market conditions. Perfect for Grandma.

Yes, it's true that the shares *can* drop down sharply in times of great economic uncertainty, or because of the financial needs of a few holders; but, as the past will show, the shares normally recover afterwards and then rise back to normal levels. If Grandma never opened her stock statement, she wouldn't know or care as the **quarterly** dividends flowed in like water for her to live off.

Definitely not exciting, these preferred shares pay between 3.5-6% on an annual basis and they have been paying dividends seemingly forever. The shares trade infrequently and are not very liquid. Grandma isn't a trader you know. Besides, Grandma isn't the only one holding these shares. Many large mutual funds and other hedge funds secretly hold onto large blocks of these, aware of their power and reliability. Neither group likes to sell and only *accumulates them* – when the prices go down.

Normally there are open bids for these shares from preferred buyers hoping to pick up some from older preferred holders who die and whose heirs sell them off looking for quick cash. The heirs haplessly have no idea what they are selling as the children of an estate get their hands on the shares and simply liquidate just for the money. It's in these moments that one can possibly acquire these shares. Morbid yes, but it is part of the circle of preferred life.

If you have an interest in getting your hands on these shares you must be patient. To do so means leaving an open order bidding for shares usually near par for long periods of time until one day out of the blue your order is filled because another grandma passed. This is the recommended way of purchasing such shares. Sure, you can buy them on the offer but that is almost always higher than par and does not contain a good amount of shares you can buy. Warning though! If you are going to attempt to buy shares on the offer you must, must, must, put in a limit order, indicating the highest price you are willing to pay for such shares. Because if you do not, the next seller of shares may be several points higher than you are wanting to pay. If you do a market order and not a limit order, I promise you will buy shares several points higher and you will be unhappy, and your brokerage firm will not normally be able to help you fix the purchase price. I have personally seen an open order on a $100 share trade at $139 because there was nothing available to buy and the makers took the market up to $139. Needless to say, the buyer was screwed and furious.

So, the question is – are grandma shares right for you? There isn't an easy answer. Clearly, there is something to be said for an investment in your local utility that pays you 5% a year and has done so for 50 years. Obviously, there is not much fear there, which is why preferred holders usually dabble in such securities.

The answer I suppose is that if you are looking for this size return and never want to look at your preferred shares and just take the dividends to use for income or to reinvest you could do that. There is a certain comfort in that as well.

Whatever your decision you have to remember these shares are not very liquid. It takes time and patience to accumulate a position in the best ones. But another advantage of them is that they can be accumulated during times of financial crisis when there are sellers in need of cashing out.

Lastly, just as accumulating these shares takes time, it could equally take time *to sell* these shares, depending on market conditions and demand from other buyers.

Examples of Grandma Shares

- 10/21/1937 CTA-B DowDuPont, Inc., $4.50 Series Cumulative 4.500% BBB
- 08/01/1941 UEPEO Union Electric Co., $4.50 Series Cumulative 4.500% Baa3 BBB-
- 10/16/1945 UELMO Union Electric Co., $3.70 Series Cumulative 3.700% Baa3 BBB-
- 01/01/1946 APRDN Alabama Power Co., 4.20% Series Cumulative 4.200% A3 BBB
- 04/30/1946 UEPEN Union Electric Co., $3.50 Series Cumulative 3.500% Baa3 BBB-
- 11/13/1946 AILLP Ameren Illinois Co., 4.00% Series Cumulative 4.000% Baa2 BBB-
- 01/01/1947 CNLTL Connecticut Light & Power Co., $1.90 Series of 1947 3.800% Baa2
- 01/01/1947 CNLTN Connecticut Light & Power Co., $2.00 Series of 1947 4.000% Baa2
- 01/20/1947 ARNC- Arconic, $3.75 Serial 3.750% BB
- 05/26/1947 CTA-A DowDuPont, Inc., $3.50 Series Cumulative 3.500% BBB
- 01/01/1949 CNLHN Connecticut Light & Power Co.,3.90% Series of 1949 3.900% Baa2
- 01/01/1949 CNLTP Connecticut Light & Power Co., $2.20 Series of 1949 4.400% Baa2
- 01/01/1949 CNPWP Connecticut Light & Power Co., $2.04 Series of 1949 4.080% Baa2
- 10/20/1949 UEPEM Union Electric Co., $4.00 Series Cumulative 4.000% Baa3 BBB-
- 01/01/1950 ALPVN Alabama Power Co., 4.60% Series Cumulative 4.600% A3 BBB

- 01/06/1950 NMK-B Niagara Mohawk Power Corp., 3.60% Series 3.600% Baa1 BBB
- 01/06/1950 NMK-C Niagara Mohawk Power Corp., 3.90% Series 3.900% Baa1 BBB
- 05/22/1950 AILIH Ameren Illinois Co., 4.08% Series Cumulative Serial 4.080% Baa2 BBB-
- 12/08/1950 AILIO Ameren Illinois Co., 4.26% Series Cumulative Serial 4.260% Baa2 BBB-
- 04/16/1952 AILIM Ameren Illinois Co., 4.70% Series Cumulative Serial 4.700% Baa2 BBB-
- 10/01/1952 AILLM Ameren Illinois Co., 4.92% Series Cumulative 4.920% Baa2 BBB-
- 03/31/1953 AILIN Ameren Illinois Co., 4.42% Series Cumulative Serial 4.420% Baa2 BBB-
- 11/01/1953 MSSEL Massachusetts Electric Co., 4.44% Series Cumulative 4.440% Baa2 BBB
- 01/01/1954 CNLPM Connecticut Light & Power Co., $2.06 Series E of 1954 4.120% Baa2
- 11/15/1954 AILIP Ameren Illinois Co., 4.20% Series Cumulative Serial 4.200% Baa2 BBB-
- 01/01/1955 CNPWM Connecticut Light & Power Co., $2.09 Series F of 1955 4.180%Baa2
- 01/01/1956 CNLHO Connecticut Light & Power Co., 4.50% Series of 1956 4.500% Baa2
- 06/13/1956 NSARP NSTAR Electric Co., 4.25% Series Cumulative 4.250%
- 01/01/1958 CNTHN Connecticut Light & Power Co., 4.96% Series of 1958 4.960% Baa2
- 07/10/1958 NSARO NSTAR Electric Co., 4.78% Series Cumulative 4.780%
- 01/01/1961 APRDM Alabama Power Co., 4.92% Series Cumulative 4.920% A3 BBB
- 11/01/1962 KSU-Kansas City Southern, 4% Non-cumulative 4.000%
- 01/01/1963 CNLHP Connecticut Light & Power Co., 4.50% Series of 1963 4.500% Baa2
- 01/01/1963 APRCP Alabama Power Co., 4.52% Series Cumulative 4.520% A3 BBB
- 05/06/1963 TY-Tri-Continental Corp., $2.50 Cumulative 5.000%
- 01/01/1964 APRDO Alabama Power Co., 4.64% Series Cumulative 4.640% A3 BBB
- 02/14/1964 UEPEP Union Electric Co., $4.56 Series Cumulative 4.560% Baa3 BBB-

- 01/01/1965 APRDP Alabama Power Co., 4.72% Series Cumulative 4.720% A3 BBB
- 01/01/1965 PNMXO Public Service Co. of New Mexico, 4.58% 1965 Series...4.580% BBB-
- 01/01/1967 CNTHO Connecticut Light & Power Co., 5.28% Series of 1967 5.280% Baa2 A-
- 01/01/1968 CNLPL Connecticut Light & Power Co., $3.24 Series G of 1968 6.480% Baa2 A-
- 01/01/1968 CNTHP Connecticut Light & Power Co., 6.56% Series of 1968 6.560% Baa2 A-
- 06/07/1968 CMS-B Consumers Energy Co., $4.50 Series Cumulative 4.500% A3
- 11/19/1975 PPWLM PacifiCorp, 7.00% Serial 7.000% Baa2 BBB+

From Grandmas to Baby-Boomers

Baby-boomers are a massive part of the American population. There are about 77 million baby boomers in the U.S.A. Are you a baby-boomer? You are if you were born between 1946 and 1964 in the post-World War II era.

According to the AARP, **10,000 baby boomers are turning 65 every single day**.

This means that nearly seven baby boomers are turning 65 every single minute.

For this reason alone, Social Security and Medicare programs are expected to run into financial trouble.

To complicate things still further, the majority of baby boomers support their adult children. According to a survey from the *National Endowment for Financial Education*, 59% of baby boomers who are parents are financially supporting their children aged 18-39.

Why does this all matter?

Because the fact is that most baby boomers are not financially prepared for retirement.

Preferred stock can often fill that gap.

24

STOCK LIQUIDITY

L IQUIDITY IN STOCKS, MEANS assets that can be easily converted into cash or liquidated without affecting that asset's price. Just look at the volume of shares that trade on a daily basis to get an idea of a stock's liquidity.

Common stock has many more buyers and sellers than preferred shares and thus are more liquid.

Preferred shares in a smaller market contain fewer buyers and sellers and are less liquid. An active common stock may trade millions of shares a day, while its preferred stock may only trade tens of thousands.

With preferred, share prices on purchase and sale often move up and down slightly. That is why it's always important to look at the volume of shares trading in a preferred security. Some trades hundreds of thousands of shares a day and others do not even open for weeks at a time.

It is also crucial to look at the **spread** or the difference in price between the bid (what you can sell for) and the ask (what you can buy shares for) of the security. **The larger the spread, the less liquid.**

Also pay attention to the size on the bid and the ask. The **size** is how much a market-maker or an investor with an open order is willing to buy or sell their shares for. The size is super important because once that amount available to be purchased or sell is gone, an illiquid security can move up or down several points at a time. If the preferred shares are not liquid, you must use limit orders only! If you do not use a limit order you could pay five or ten points more for a share as there may be nothing between the shares shown and others much higher for sale and you do not want to be taken advantage of by an unscrupulous market-maker. This often occurs in the trading of grandma shares.

25

FLIPPING AND CLIPPING AND FRONT RUNNING

"Everything counts in large amounts"
– Depeche Mode

THE TERM "FLIPPING", IS Wall Street slang for a practice whereby investors quickly resell shares of a new offering of stock called an "Initial Public Offering" or "IPO" they just purchased.

The flipper buys the shares looking for a pop up in the price of the security in the first few minutes or hours then sells all to earn a quick profit.

The goal of the flipper generally rides on the short-term volatility of the IPO in the hopes of making fast cash. The flipper banks on the idea that first the underwriters of the IPO have underpriced the security *just enough* that it will, at a minimum, have a small pop up in price at the opening and, second, that the underwriters themselves will hold the IPO price per share at the IPO issuance price, creating a temporary floor, so that security price closes at or above its issuance price.

The underwriters do this to make sure that clients buying the IPO pay for the securities ordered and there is no better way to assure that the shares are paid for than having them worth more on the first day of trading.

Underwriters, in an effort to *prevent* flipping, try to place IPO stock in the hands of long-term investors. They typically have an unspoken practice of specifically targeting those investors that promise aftermarket orders of the IPO stock. The thought being that if the investor is willing to buy additional shares in the open market (which are often higher than the IPO price, apart from those shares allotted to them at the IPO price) then they will be holders. The logic behind this practice is that investors who are holders who try to sell immediately would incur a loss.

Flipping Preferred

While not nearly as well-known as a common stock IPO flips, flipping new issues of preferred shares can offer a similar opportunity but with much greater safety. Today, most new issues of preferred stock are priced and issued at $25 per share with many of them beginning trading initially, as wholesaled and discounted on the Over-The-Counter market. These preferred issues begin trading at random times of the day selected by the underwriter, so most people have no idea when they are about to begin to trade.

Most preferred shares begin their life trading on the OTC market which gives the flipper of preferred an additional advantage to the common stock flipper in that the shares can often be bought below par of $25 or below IPO price. Sometimes the discounted price could be just a few pennies, other times depending on market conditions, up to $0.50 below. This discount may linger until the shares are moved up the listing on the NYSE or other exchange. Once the listing is lifted to a major exchange, the shares will often move up in price though this depends on demand.

What Makes Flipping Preferred Desirable?

The major difference in flipping preferred shares versus a common stock IPO is the initial quality of the preferred shares. With a common stock IPO, the underwriters will often **hold** the bid, creating a **floor** until all shares are paid for. Once the underwriter steps away, where the shares go is anyone's guess.

Let's look at the *Facebook* IPO and see what happened as soon as the underwriters stepped away.

The social networking company *Facebook* held its initial public offering (IPO) on Friday, May 18, 2012. The $38 per share IPO was the biggest in technology and Internet history, with a peak market capitalization of over $104 billion.

First Day

An electronic billboard on the Thompson Reuters building welcomes Facebook to the NASDAQ.

- Trading was to begin at 11:00am Eastern Time on Friday, May 18, 2012.
- Trading was delayed until 11:30am Eastern Time due to technical problems with the NASDAQ exchange.
- Initial trading saw the stock shoot up to as much as $45.
- IPO flippers flooded the market with shares, forcing underwriters to buy back shares to support the price.
- Only the underwriter support prevented the stock price from falling below the IPO price on the first day of trading.
- At closing bell, shares were valued at $38.23, only $0.23 above the IPO price, down $3.82 from the opening bell.
- The underwriters were paid, and IPO trades closed out and then the underwriter stepped away.
- *Facebook*'s share value fell during nine of the next thirteen trading days.

- The next day of trading after the IPO (May 21), the stock closed at $34.03.
- The stock saw another large loss the next day, closing at $31.00.
- A circuit breaker was used to slow down the decline in the stock price.
- The stock returned to losses for most of its second full week and had lost over a quarter of its starting value by the end of May.
- The stock closed its second full week of trading on June 1 at $27.72.
- By June 6 investors had lost $40 billion.
- Facebook ended its third full week at $27.10, slightly lower than a week previous.

Facebook

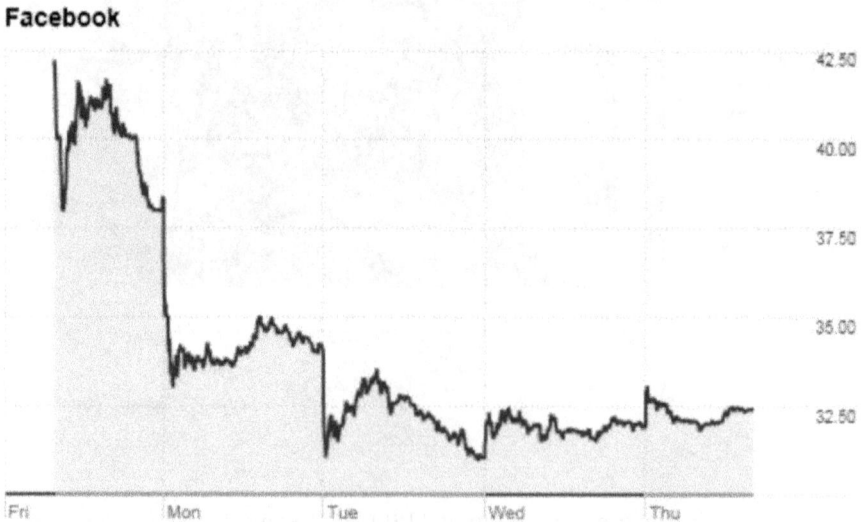

Figure 24

Why This Is Not an Issue for Preferred IPO Flips

The *Facebook* IPO serves as a great example for everything that can go wrong with a typical common stock IPO. The initial problem with the *Facebook* IPO was that it was too large a deal for a company that wasn't making money.

Because of its size, the underwriters had a hard time placing the stock and instead of placing it in the hands of long-term holders it sold the shares to anyone regardless if they agreed to buy additional after market shares or not.

This led to just about every flipper getting their hands on as many shares as they could. Worse, there were other investors who had held *Facebook* stock who were able to sell at the IPO.

Once the IPO began trading it was a mad rush for the door by everyone. The flippers sold as quickly as they could. The investors who could sell and insiders who could sell also sold.

The underwriter held the shares at the IPO price to make sure they were paid for. Once the trading day was over and the shares were paid for the next day the underwriter stopped holding the price up and the stock dropped 30%.

Why Doesn't This Happen with a Preferred Stock IPO?

For preferred IPO's, while the basic idea is the same, being a new issuance of shares, the major differences lie in the details.

Yes, new shares are brought to market, but the buyers of these shares are institutions and funds looking to hold long-term. When sold to individual investors most brokerage firms typically limit the amount of preferred shares to be sold to range between one thousand to five thousand shares. With small allocations no one share purchaser can wreak havoc or collapse the price. This is important to the underwriter of a new preferred issuer because, unlike a common stock IPO where the money raised goes to the issuer, in a preferred offering the underwriter normally puts up all the cash up front and only recoups that capital plus their profit upon successful sale of the preferred IPO.

With the underwriter's cash at risk in a preferred offering, the underwriter is careful who they sell the offering to, so as to be assured of repayment. This results in a stable after-IPO price 99% of the time.

Underwriters of a preferred IPO don't have to fear insider selling or investor selling as there are no insiders or investors at the preferred level, unlike with common shares. The preferred IPO is also different to a common stock IPO in that the majority of the companies raising capital are large, better known, money-making institutions who pay dividends; rather than companies who may not be profitable.

Being profitable entities eliminates fear of the company going out of business immediately after the offering.

Lastly, flippers in preferred are not the norm as immediate pops are less frequent and much smaller. Most investors are in for the long term and the preferred IPO flipper is mostly an outlier as most choose to hold through the dividend.

What Makes a Good Flip and How Does it Work?

Throughout this book we have established what makes a preferred desirable as a holding for the long-term, and what we would like to avoid.

Normally, preferred shares we look to hold are:

- American
- Profitable
- Large
- Strong underwriter
- Strong credit rating
- Dividend rate over 6%
- History and track record
- Cumulative dividends
- Dividends paid quarterly
- Non-convertible preferred
- Callable in five years
- Fixed rate, not variable rate preferred

But what about a preferred stock for flipping?
Which preferred stocks make the best flip candidates?

Flip candidates we look for:

- American or foreign
- Profitable
- Large
- First dividend shorter than 90 days. (The shorter time till the first dividend the better.)
- Strong underwriter
- Strong credit rating
- Higher than normal dividend rate
- History and track record
- Fixed rate or variable rate preferred

What we don't flip:

- Small small deals
- No name underwriters

- Those that never made money
- First-timers to market
- Losing money
- Risky industry
- Hard for underwriter to sell

Today, issues with coupons greater than 6% are of most interest to a flipper and most are seeing an immediate spike in trading. Many move higher within a week of being listed on a major exchange like the NYSE from the OTC. Some move $0.25 higher while others move up 1-2 points.

Often flippers will buy a larger amount of shares at $25 or below and then sell them higher. Again, it's not monster gains but on 10,000 shares a flipper can earn $10-20,000 or 4-8% with little effort unloading the shares in 1, 3, 5 or 15 days. Unlike a common stock IPO where anything can happen, most preferred sold are safe in that they are higher quality issues that just took in an enormous amount of cash, greatly reducing the immediate downside to the flipper.

Very few preferred **break bid**, meaning they don't close lower than the first discounted trade on the OTC market or $25 if listed directly on the NYSE. This limited downside and strong potential for upside has sophisticated traders quietly flipping preferred.

Flipping High Rate - Less Desirable Preferred Shares

There are preferred shares others want to buy for higher rates, but to us and our plan these are not desirable as they are less stable, or non-cumulative, etc. But in low interest markets, investors and funds gobble up these high payers to spike their returns. Often these investors and funds pay up for the rate and *this is where you can catch a free ride*. You can catch a 4-8 % return on cap gain alone.

So, what makes a good flip Let's look at two to see why one appreciated more than the other.

First factor: how close is that first dividend? The closer in time, the better. So on a preferred paying 7%, the annual dividend is X and quarterly is X so hypothetically if the first dividend is 30 or 45 days later you know this fresh-funded preferred is going to payout $X per share.

That being the case, based on the behavior of preferred shares, in 30-45 days what price would you roughly guess the preferred to be trading near? If you said $25.X or $25 plus the bounty attached to the preferred you'd be right!

As a flipper, $0.43 per share gain or so on 10,000 shares would give you a pretty $4300! Not a bad return on a flip. As the band *Depeche Mode* sang, *everything counts in large amounts.*

You can buy in wholesale markets, circumventing the underwriters – their fear of selling the units to get cash back is **your secret weapon** to getting the IPO flip size you need. The underwriter doesn't have the time to wait.

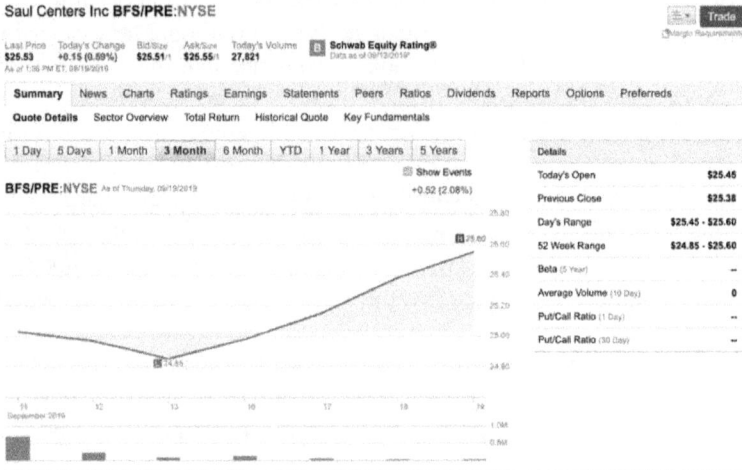

Figure 25 Rises to flip price

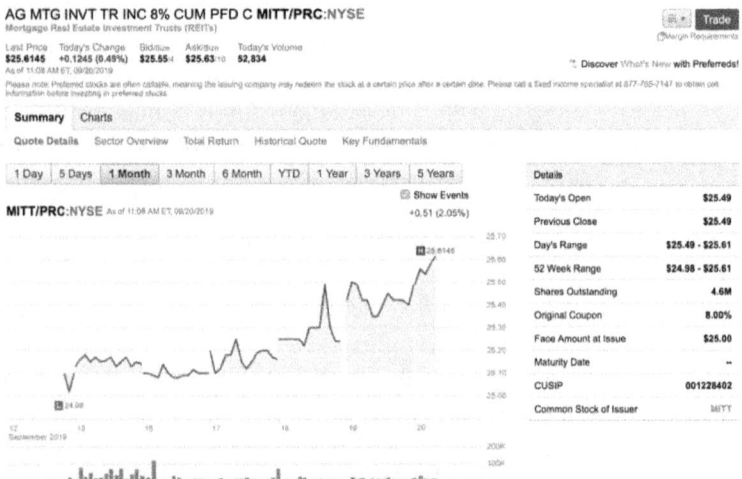

Figure 26

26
SELLING

WHEN BUYING AND SELLING preferred shares it is important to know that preferred shares can be less liquid than most common shares. Selling and buying preferred sometimes means paying a little more for shares or getting a little less when selling shares depending on their liquidity. For these reasons it is important to understand how preferred are traded, what to look for and how to use a level 2 system when trading.

Many Preferred Stocks Are Thinly Traded

Many preferred shares cannot be easily sold without affecting the price, as preferred shares are often traded in lower volumes and have fewer buyers and sellers. Fewer traders may cause changes in price when a transaction does occur. The lack of ready buyers and sellers can lead to large disparities between the **bid** and the **ask price**. When a seller sells at the bid or a buyer buys at the ask, the price of the security can **experience a move**. Thinly-traded securities are usually more risky because the small number of market participants can impact the price, called **liquidity risk**.

Quick Ways to Determine If a Preferred Is Thinly Traded:

- Dollar volume: Look how many U.S. dollars are traded per day. Preferred with low dollar volumes may be more thinly-traded than those with higher dollar volumes.
- Bid-ask spread: The difference between the bid and ask price is called **the spread**. When you see a big spread, think less liquidity! The **bid-ask spread** is basically the difference between the highest price that a buyer is willing to pay for a preferred share and the lowest price that a seller is willing to accept. An individual looking to sell will receive the bid price while one looking to buy will pay the ask price.

Selling Thinly Traded Preferred Quickly Could Cause a Loss

Selling thinly-traded preferred may cause a loss if the preferred shares are needed to be sold quickly as there may not be a ready supply of buyers to buy the shares. In more extreme cases, it may not be possible to sell the security without a large loss or at all. Because some shares are thinly-traded, the price of many preferred stocks tend to be more volatile.

What Is Level 2?

Level 2 is the electronic order book, a list of buy and sell orders for a stock organized by price level. The order book lists the number of shares being **bid for** (looking to be bought) or **offered out** (looking to be sold) at each price level known as '**the market depth**'.

The level 2 order book lists the market makers, by company name, behind the buy and sell orders. With these transactions, known as **principal trades**, market makers enter and change quotes to buy, sell, execute or clear orders. When orders are placed, they are placed through firms that make a market (the market makers) in the security.

Level 2 is helpful in providing a view into a preferred stock's price movement, showing what type of traders are buying or selling and where the stock could head over the short term.

Let's look at the different market makers possible.

There are three different types of makers in the marketplace:

1. Market Makers (MM) – They make the market, meaning that they are required to quote to buy when nobody else is buying and post to sell when nobody else is selling.
2. Electronic Communication Networks (ECN) – Electronic communication networks are computerized order placement systems. Sometimes an order you place to buy will be routed to an ECN. Anyone or any entity can trade through ECNs.
3. Wholesalers (order flow firms) – Many online brokers sell their order flow to wholesalers; who then execute the orders on behalf of the online brokers and their retail trader's clients.

Market makers must commit to continuously quote prices at which they will buy (or bid) and sell (or ask) securities. Market makers must also quote the minimum amount in which they're willing to trade. Market makers must stick to these parameters at all times. If a market maker violates these rules not honoring a quote (it still happens, but not frequently) it is called **backing away**.

The Level 2's value lies in showing you a ranked list of the best bid and ask prices from each maker participant, giving you a detailed insight into the price action. With this knowledge you can determine how many shares could be bought or sold without affecting the market. Knowing exactly who has an interest in a stock and how much they may want to buy or sell is useful for seeing exactly where buying and selling amounts are placed.

This is what a level 2 quote looks like:

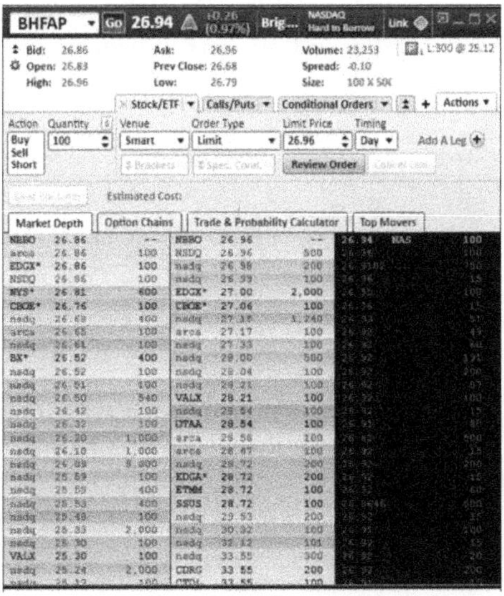

Figure 27

This tells us that *ARCA, EDGX, NSDQ Securities* are looking to buy 100 shares each of stock at a price of $26.86 and that *NSDQ Securities* is looking to sell 500 shares of stock at a price of $26.96. Now let's take a look at the main market participant…

The Ax

This is important. The ax is the one market maker that controls the price action in a given stock. To find the ax simply watch the movement on the level 2 for a few days. The market maker who consistently dominates the price action, he or she's the ax.

Why Use Level 2?

Level 2 quotes can give you a view into what's happening with a stock:

- For instance, you can tell the kind of buying (whether retail or institutional) just by looking at the market makers involved. Large institutions typically use different market makers than retail traders.
- Look for irregular ECN order size buys which is a 'tell' for when institutions are trying to accumulate a larger amount of shares.
- Watch trading by the ax when the price is rising or declining as the ax provides liquidity and projects direction.

Market Maker Trickery

While watching the level 2 can hint at what is happening, there is also a lot of **trickery**. Common tricks played by market makers are:

- Hiding order sizes – market makers regularly post smaller order sizes on the bid and on the offer than the actual order they hold. This is meant as a ruse so not to tip off other traders (if buying) or scare them off (when selling). The thinking here is that no one is going to try to push through a large block of shares, eg. 100,000 shares, all at once, but if a smaller 10,000 share amount appeared on the offer, traders may think that taking that offer may lift that offer to the next price level. Alternatively, a large bid for shares if not disguised as something smaller, *might* cause a run on the stock as traders see a large bid size for the stock as someone looking to buy many shares.

- Market makers may hide their actions trading through ECNs. Again, ECNs can be used by anyone, so it is often difficult to tell whether large ECN orders are retail or institutional.

The bottom line is this: use of a Level 2 can give you an insight into a stock's price action, but market makers can also do things to disguise their true intentions.

27

BUYING WITH A CUSIP

FROM TIME-TO-TIME a new preferred stock will come to market, trading OTC, listed only by its **CUSIP number**. Whether you know it or not, issuers of new preferred shares would rather trade just by CUSIP as the CUSIP number can identify a publicly traded security *precisely*, ensuring proper categorization of the security purchase. This ensures your securities trades are processed, cleared and settled correctly.

Essentially, trading by CUSIP makes life easier for any party attached to a securities settlement and that's why many preferred shares start their lives trading initially by CUSIP.

Don't fret: you can still trade a new preferred stock just by using its **CUSIP number. All it takes is an old-fashioned phone call**. I have learned that it's actually even easier to trade a new preferred by CUSIP number rather than a stock symbol, as many brokerage firms are reluctant to trade the temporary symbol. Just know that following the initial trading, the CUSIP number will eventually give way to a permanent stock symbol, which will then be used when the security is uplisted from the OTC to its final trading exchange.

What is a CUSIP and What Does It Mean?

A CUSIP number is a series of numbers and letters used by Wall Street to identify an investment security. Think of CUSIP numbers and letters as Wall Street's **"bar codes"** or "**QR codes**" – identifiers to designate, record and document the trade.

CUSIP itself stands for **Committee on Uniform Securities Identification Procedures**. It identifies all registered United States publicly traded companies and all United States government and municipal bonds including preferred stock and even CD's.

What's the Difference Between a Ticker Symbol and a CUSIP Number?

While both a CUSIP and stock symbol both identify publicly traded securities, that's where the similarity ends. Understand that a **stock symbol** is used on the **front end of a trade**, to identify the stock a buyer may want to buy but then the **CUSIP** number's job comes into play **at the actual purchase** with the CUSIP number as part of the trade confirmation to cause the securities trades to be processed, cleared and settled.

Ownership and History

The CUSIP system dates back to 1955 and is owned by the American Bankers Association and is operated by *S&P Global*. Today the CUSIP system holds data on 44 million financial instruments making it one of the largest holders of financial and investment data in the world.

What a CUSIP Number Looks Like

A CUSIP number includes nine characters that may have both letters and numbers. Each CUSIP number offers a formula for the security including the company or issuer and the type of investment security being a stock, bond or fund. The first six characters in a CUSIP are the *base identifiers* of the security's issuer, while the seventh and eighth characters identify the type of security. The last component, the ninth character, is called the *check digit* and isn't always used to clear or settle a trade.

How Are CUSIP Numbers Assigned?

CUSIP numbers are assigned following an application to *CUSIP Global Services*, the administrative organization that handles the distribution of CUSIP numbers.

Finding a CUSIP on a New Preferred Stock

The easiest way to find the CUSIP number on a new preferred stock is on the FWP or Free Writing Prospectus or Stock Term sheet listed on the SEC.gov website prior to the trading of the security. It's also available from your broker. The CUSIP number is at the bottom of the FWP.

Other Ways to Find a CUSIP Number

Another way to get your securities CUSIP number is through a basic *Google* search. For instance, type in "Ford CUSIP" on *Google* and you'll be led to its CUSIP number. But sometimes the CUSIP number is not easy to find on a new or specific strain of stock like that of preferred stock and ETD. In that case, just call your broker or brokerage. You could also get a copy of your security's physical stock certificate or call the company's stock transfer agent.

Trading Using Just the CUSIP Number

To place a trade on a new preferred security just call your broker or online brokerage firm's **trading desk**. Once you go through all the formalities regarding your account, tell the broker you would like to purchase the preferred and tell the trader the CUSIP number. The trader will be able to find the security easily and place the trade.

In a situation like this the security will appear as a CUSIP number on your statement until the time whereby the security is given a temporary or permanent stock symbol. At that time the statement will change to reflect the new stock symbol.

Section 1: FWP (FWP)

Filed Pursuant to Rule 433
Registration No. 333-212916
June 24, 2019

Synovus Financial Corp.

14,000,000 Underwritten Shares of 5.875%
Fixed-Rate Reset Non-Cumulative Perpetual Preferred Stock, Series E ("Series E Preferred Stock")

Issuer:	Synovus Financial Corp. (the "Company"), a Georgia corporation.
Securities Offered:	14,000,000 shares of Series E Preferred Stock, with no over-allotment option
Liquidation Preference:	$25 per share of Series E Preferred Stock
Maturity Date:	Perpetual
First Call Date	July 1, 2024
Reset Date	The First Call Date and each date falling on the fifth anniversary of the preceding reset date.
Reset Period	The period from and including the First Call Date to, but excluding, the next following Reset Date and thereafter each period from and including each Reset Date to, but excluding, the next following Reset Date.
Dividend Rate (Non-Cumulative):	(1) 5.875% per annum from the issue date of the shares of the Series E Preferred Stock to, but excluding, the First Call Date; and
	(2) the Five-year U.S. Treasury Rate (as defined in the preliminary prospectus supplement) as of the most recent reset dividend determination date (as defined in the preliminary prospectus supplement) plus 4.127% per annum, for each Reset Period from and including the First Call Date.
Dividend Payment Dates:	Beginning October 1, 2019, each January 1, April 1, July 1 and October 1
Day Count:	30/360
Optional Redemption:	Redeemable, at the option of the Company, (i) in whole or in part, from time to time, on the First Call Date or any subsequent Reset Date, or (ii) in whole but not in part, at any time within 90 days following a regulatory capital treatment event (as defined in the preliminary prospectus supplement), in each case at a redemption price equal to $25 per share, plus any declared and unpaid dividends, without accumulation of any undeclared dividends.

Trade Date:	June 24, 2019
Settlement Date:	July 1, 2019
Public Offering Price:	$25 per Underwritten Share
Underwriting Commission:	For all sales, except to institutions, 3.150%; for sales to institutions, 2.000%
Net Proceeds (before expenses) to the Issuer:	$342,022,500
Bookrunning Managers:	BofA Securities, Inc. J.P. Morgan Securities LLC
Co-Managers:	Sandler O'Neill + Partners, L.P. Synovus Securities, Inc.
CUSIP/ISIN:	87161C 709 / US87161C7092

Figure 28 FWP showing CUSIP bottom left

28

YIELD CURVES

"The trend is your friend, until the end when it bends."
– Ed Seykota

THE YIELD CURVE MEASURES how investors feel about risk. The yield curve shows the short, intermediate, and long-term rates of US Treasury securities. To be a strong preferred investor you must watch and react to yield and the yield curve as yields change. Understand that, if the downward trend continues, American yields appear to be heading lower as we are virtually the last man standing of any major market with positive yields.

While this may be a great time for the individual borrower as mortgage rates drop, for **fixed-income investors** it's a totally different story. With very low yields, or no yields across the planet **the "Boom" for borrowers is a "Bust" for those living off yield**, including retirees, seniors and any other individuals that live off of their incomes.

A Normal Yield Curve

With a normal yield curve, short-term securities carry lower yields reflecting that an investor's money is less at risk. This is shown in the normal yield curve, sloping upward from left to right on the graph as maturities lengthen and yields rise.

NORMAL YIELD CURVE

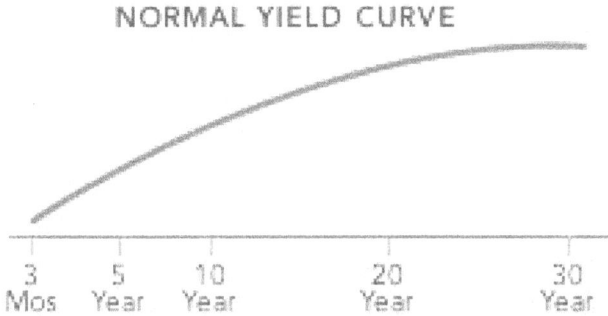

| 3 | 5 | 10 | 20 | 30 |
| Mos | Year | Year | Year | Year |

For illustrative purposes only.

Figure 29

This type of yield curve is when bond investors expect the economy to grow normally, without significant changes in the inflation rate or interruptions to available credit. When the curve's shape changes though, watch for potential turning points in the economy.

As a preferred investor we must watch the yield curve closely as it will influence our decisions on buying or selling. The rule to remember is "The trend is your friend, until the end when it bends." In other words, keep following the trend until the trend stops and reverses course! The trick with buying preferred stock is to be patient through the small changes in yield until the time you can see the actual point, the pivot, when the trend makes a change in direction or "bends." Once the bend occurs be prepared to change strategy on your preferred investments following the new trend.

The Trend is Your Friend, Until the End When it Bends

10 Year Treasury Rate - 54 Year Historical Chart

Below is an interactive chart showing the daily ten-year treasury yield back to 1962. The shaded areas show recessions. The ten-year treasury is the benchmark used to decide mortgage rates across the U.S. and is the most liquid and widely-traded bond in the world. The current ten-year treasury yield as of September 04, 2019 is 1.47%.

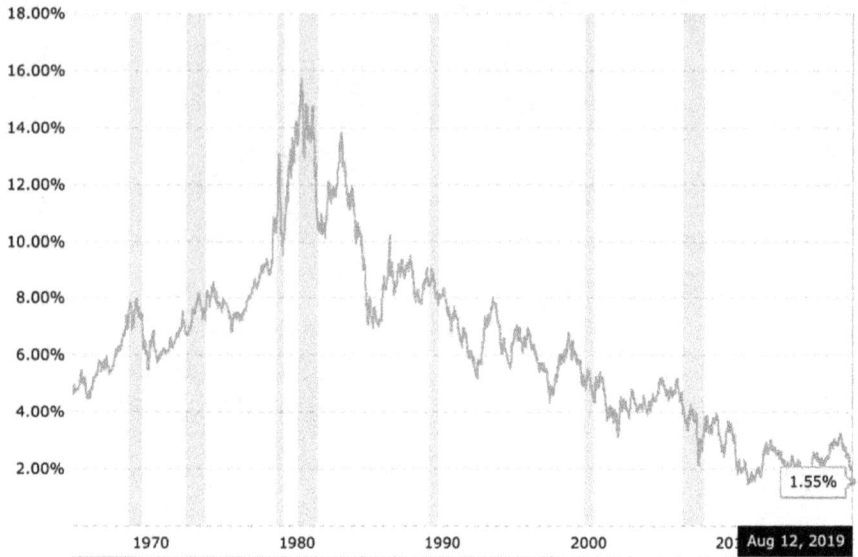

Figure 30

10 Year Treasury Rate - 20 Year Historical Chart

Below is a twenty-year interactive chart showing the daily ten-year treasury yield back to 1999. The shaded areas show recessions.

7.00%
6.50%
6.00%
5.50%
5.00%
4.50%
4.00%
3.50%
3.00%
2.50%
2.00%
1.50%

2000 2002 2004 2006 2008 2010 2012 2014 201 **Aug 26, 2019**

1.50%

Figure 31

What we can clearly see from both charts is that the ten-year treasury has been on a meandering path of decline for roughly forty years. A strong example of an overall downward trend! Sure, there have been periods of small treasury rate increases, but rates in general have trended downward for decades. If you have heard the saying 'the trend is your friend until the end when it bends' you understand that as an investor you cannot fight the movement by federal reserve or you will lose. Until the time comes where the trend returns to a normal yield curve (the bend) from a negative yield curve, continue to invest as if rates are going lower.

What's an Inverted Yield Curve and What's Its Importance?

An inverted yield curve, or negative yield curve, is when long-term debt yields less than short-term debt.

The whole idea of the inverted yield curve seems counterintuitive.

Why would long-term investors accept lower rewards than short-term investors, who assume less risk?

The answer: when long-term investors feel that this is their last shot to lock in current rates before they fall lower!

Lower interest rates suggest slower economic growth, and an inverted yield curve is viewed as a sign that the economy may stagnate. While inverted yield curves are uncommon, don't ignore them as they are often followed by lower interest rates along all points of the yield curve.

As we can see below, as of September 5, 2019, U.S. Treasuries have almost fully inverted with the 3-month U.S. Treasury paying 2% while the 10-year pays almost half a point lower at 1.56%. This is opposite the norm (see chart) as yields are normally higher on fixed-income securities with longer maturity dates.

Higher yields on longer-term securities are a result of a maturity risk premium on fixed-income securities with longer maturity dates, as longer-term securities are more unpredictable over a longer time horizon.

Fixed Income Offerings POWERED BY **BondSource**™

	3 Mo	6 Mo	9 Mo	1 Yr	2 Yr	3 Yr	5 Yr	10 Yr	20 Yr	30 Yr+
CDs	1.96	1.85	1.80	1.85	1.90	2.00	2.15	2.52	--	--
Bonds										
U.S. Treasuries	2.00	1.88	1.79	1.74	1.55	1.45	1.44	1.56	1.86	2.04

Figure 32

When viewed as a graph you can straightaway see why it's called a negative or inverted yield curve:

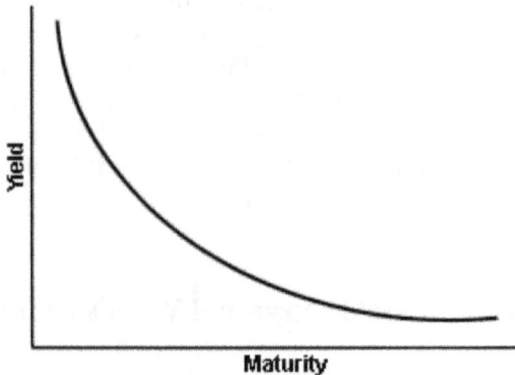

Figure 33

What Does This Mean for the Preferred Investor?

It's often been said that **the shape of the yield curve changes in accordance with the state of the economy**. An upward-sloped yield curve is normal when the economy is growing. Conversely, the inverted or down-sloped yield curve is associated with an economy in, or entering into, a recession.

The reason a relationship exists between the yield and the economy's performance relates to how higher or lower levels of long-term capital investment grows or retracts the economy.

Jumpstarting

When businesses and governments need investment capital at affordable costs to **jump start a weak economy**, they do it by issuing longer-term securities with lower-yield offerings.

Yields are moved in the market by demands for securities of different maturities at a particular time and under given economic conditions. When the economy is heading to a recession, knowing interest rates are to trend lower, investors are more willing to invest in longer-term securities immediately to lock in current higher yields.

This, in turn, increases the demand for longer-term securities, boosting their prices and further lowering their yields.

Meanwhile, few investors want to invest in shorter-term securities when presented with lower reinvestment rates. With lower demand for shorter-term securities, their yields actually go up, giving rise to an inverted yield curve when yields on longer-term securities have come down at the same time.

However, yields on longer-term securities could be trending down when market interest rates are set to get lower for a foreseeable future, to accommodate ongoing weak economic activities. **Irrespective of their reinvestment rate risk, shorter-term securities appear to offer higher returns than longer-term securities during such times.**

When to Pivot

In other words, how do you tell when to enter and exit the market? First, know that we are investors with our money, not traders. Nonetheless there may be times, as we have seen, that we need to make a decision to sell.

Remember our grandma shares? Long-term investment in preferred stock mostly eliminates the need for knee-jerk reactions! Grandma didn't notice or care about the intermediate ups and down of her shares.

Also, this book started with the observation that, unlike common shareholders, preferred shareholders DO NOT need to panic and sell when markets take a downturn as these can sometimes be opportunities for increasing profit. We really can profit from low rate turnarounds, just as

floaters' variable rates can profit from a rate rise. To make huge capital gains, buy when rates go to zero. This is a sign that corporations are refinancing before borrowing costs rise significantly.

Preferred shares trade just like regular shares of common stock. Some days they go up and other days they go down. Typically, quality preferred shares which pay over 6% are in demand. Often a 6% dividend, $25 preferred, purchased as a new issue over a period of time will attract buyers causing the price per share of that preferred to increase. Now follow me on this. If that preferred share price goes up just one point from $25 to $26 of just $1 per share that $1 increase in share price equals 4%. This sale of stock to get the additional $1 is called "downstream income" and it occurs regularly with quality preferred shares. Now had you held that 6%, $25 preferred for a year you would have earned in dividends $1.50 per share or 6% and then if you were then able to then sell that preferred for $26 per share you would earn $1 or 4% in capital gains or your downstream income which would give you a 10% return for the year or 6% + 4%= 10%. This is not an imaginary situation. It happens - everyday. Best, it's not rocket science either.

But what happens if the share prices rises to $27 or $2 above your purchase price of $25 per share?

Well, those two points of downstream income, upon sale, equal an 8% return (2 points divided by 25 = 8%). if you add a year of dividends to your downstream income your total return jumps to 14% or 6% plus 8%. That's how you can earn 10-15% a year on quality preferred stocks.

Compound Interest

While the term compound interest sounds complex, all it really means is interest-on-interest. Interest compounding is merely the result of **reinvesting** that new interest you have recently earned, rather than taking it out. So, if you reinvest that recently earned interest (or accumulated interest) you will now earn interest not only on your principal but your principal plus that new interest, hence compounding your result.

When we have preferred stock and we reinvest that interest over a period of years, or quarterly, we can compound the return.

What to Do in the Last Year

You bought the preferred shares four years ago. You have collected four years of dividends. The preferred trades at a premium; maybe 4% at 26. But, as they now come into the fifth year, or the year they will be called, the shares are coming down monthly a few cents here and there. What do you do?

This is a dilemma that often faces preferred holders. Do you hold until the end and get called or sell now in advance?

The stock is moving down for a reason. With each day that goes by the amount owed in dividends decreases. Each quarter that a dividend is paid is one less to collect. With one year, left one year's worth of dividend is remaining to be paid. So, let's use a 4% preferred as an easy example.

A 4% preferred pays $1 a year or $0.25 per quarter in dividends. As each quarter dividend is paid we can assume the preferred shares will decline $0.25 per quarter as the preferred has given up that quarter's bounty. Now, if we felt that thus 4% preferred was going to be called because rates had fallen to 3% then **we have to decide to sell or hold till call**.

If would be reasonable to believe that a $25 4% preferred could be trading at $26 with one year left, seeing as it still contains $1 in dividends. At a $1 premium of $26 over $25 you can take the $1 now rather than wait. More often than not it's the move to make, as you can then reinvest that early dollar earned **in another preferred for the year** and **double dip**: getting your 4% upfront and maybe a new 4% in a new preferred.

What If the Market Crashes?

In a massive crash, preferred shares of all shapes and styles will decline. It doesn't matter if they are great good or bad: all will fall. To what extent depends on the severity of the crash. Why? Simple, during crashes fear, need of cash and margin calls all cause shares to be dumped.

This dumping creates opportunities. Regardless of the reason, these are often the best times to buy. Remember unlike common shares, quality preferred shares become more valuable as they become cheaper as yields climb based on purchase price and **purchasing below par** creates **fantastic opportunities for capital gains** on call.

Let's look at examples during the last crash...

One of the nice things about preferred shares is after a crash there is a short period of time to accumulate shares before the share prices of the surviving companies return to normal. In a crash we see the downturn in share prices, followed by a leveling out, and then a *hockey stick* when the shares move back up to normal.

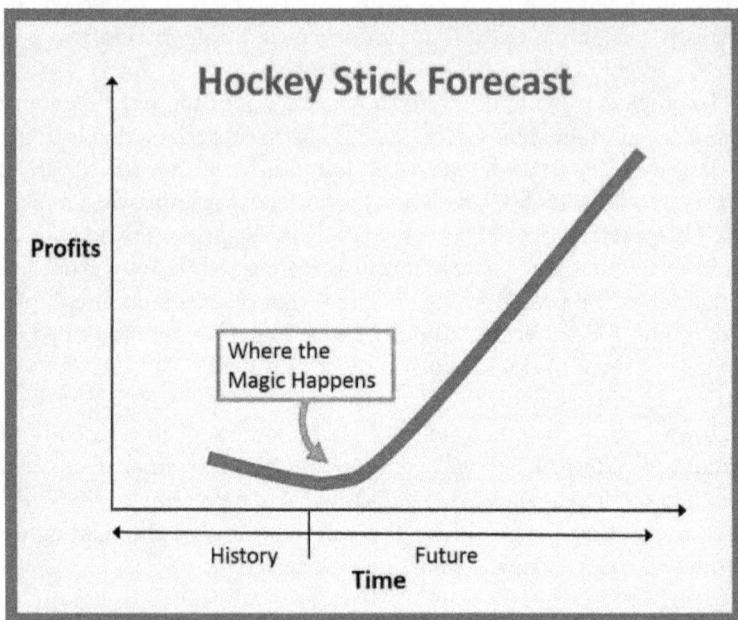

Figure 34

People often say regarding this theory, *that was in the past… why should we believe the same will happen in the future?* I used to get annoyed by this question but I understand why people ask it. Fear. My answer comes in the form of a question.

I ask *"do you feel the United States and its economy have failed beyond repair and will not recover? If your answer is yes then you should not invest any further. If your answer is no and you believe that the United States will come back then you should invest."*

Warren Buffet said it best – "It's never paid to bet against America. We come through things, but it's not always a smooth ride".

A significant part of Warren Buffett's enormous financial success is built on the money he's put behind his unwavering belief that America's brand of capitalism, from the earliest days of its founding, has fueled ever-growing prosperity for its businesses and its people, **and that it will continue to do so far into the future**. With preferred shares it is no different.

29

ASSET-BACKING STRATS

S TRATS WERE FIRST DEVELOPED by *Wachovia* in 2005, whereby investors purchasing STRATS were actually **buying shares in a trust** that pays income based upon the trust's interest in a capital security **plus a derivative product**.

The derivative here is a security with a value that is 'derived' from an underlying asset or group of assets. The derivative part is basically a contract between two or more parties that **derives its price from fluctuations in the underlying asset**.

The most common underlying assets for derivatives are stocks, bonds, commodities, currencies, interest rates, and market indexes.

With STRATS, a trust repackages an asset-backed security (ABS) or a financial security such as a bond or note collateralized by a group of assets – such as bonds or notes backed by an underlying asset. The trust then combines those securities with a derivative, being an interest rate swap to **hedge against interest rate risk** in the security component. The trust bases its payments to investors on the income streams derived **from the two** components.

To avoid such negative surprises, retail investors should always research investment products to ensure they understand all their elements and read the **prospectus** carefully before committing to an investment.

Understanding Asset-Backed Securities

Asset-backed securities allow issuers to generate more cash, which, in turn, is used for more lending, while giving investors the opportunity to invest in a wide variety of income-generating assets. Usually, the underlying assets of an ABS are **illiquid** and can't be sold on their own. However, pooling the assets together and **creating a financial security**, a process called **securitization**, enables the owner of the assets to make them marketable.

The underlying assets of these pools may be home equity loans, automobile loans, credit card receivables, student loans, or other expected cash flows. Issuers of ABS can be as creative as they desire. For example, ABS have been created based on cash flows from movie revenues, royalty payments, aircraft leases, and solar photovoltaics. Just about any cash-producing situation can be securitized into an ABS.

ABC's of an ABS

Assume that *Company X* is in the business of making automobile loans. If a person wants to borrow money to buy a car, *Company X* gives that person the cash, and the person is obligated to repay the loan with a certain amount of interest. Perhaps *Company X* makes so many loans that it runs out of cash to continue making more loans. It can then package its current loans and sell them to *Investment Firm X*, thus receiving cash that it can use to make more loans.

Investment Firm X will then sort the purchased loans into different groups called **tranches**. These tranches are groups of loans with similar characteristics, such as maturity, interest rate, and expected delinquency rate. Next, *Investment Firm X* will issue securities that are similar to typical bonds on each tranche it creates.

Individual investors then purchase these securities and receive the cash-flows from the underlying pool of auto loans, minus an administrative fee that *Investment Firm X* keeps for itself.

Tranches

An ABS will usually have three tranches: classes A, B and C. The senior tranche, A, is almost always the largest tranche and is structured to have an investment-grade rating to make it attractive to investors.

The B tranche has lower credit quality and thus has a higher yield than the senior tranche. The C tranche has a lower credit rating than the B tranche and might have such poor credit quality that it can't be sold to investors. In this case, the issuer would keep the C tranche and absorb the losses.

30

WAYS TO WIN

IF YOU WANT ACCESS to new preferred shares you need to open minimally **one or two big name** brokerage accounts. By big name I mean *Morgan Stanley, Bank of America/Merrill Lynch, Goldman Sachs,* types. Why?

Well, not all new preferred issues initially trade the same way. Yes, most will initially list first on the wholesale market, on the OTC market as discussed previously, but **some do not**.

Others, like a recent ETD issue of *Ford 6.2% Preferred A* were sold directly to customers of the underwriting firm, *Bank of America/Merrill Lynch* and its syndicate. That meant only brokerage firms' customers had access to the shares. With the Ford ETDS there was no trading on the OTC market. Instead the shares waited out the listing period in hibernation only to list directly on the NYSE.

When the shares opened for trading the first trades were well above the $25 offering price. If you did not have an account with one of the firms offering the shares you would have been shut out and would have had to pay up handsomely, initially. With issues in large demand this could be the difference in buying the offering or passing on it – as the premium to purchase would be too high to make sense. **Some of the best offerings come direct** and you as a preferred investor do not want to miss out on the best, do you?

There is another great reason why having a big brokerage firm account is special for preferred stock purchasers. No commissions. The nice thing about buying shares with a large name firm is that as long as the account is merely a brokerage account and not a managed account (where you pay a portion of the accounts balance as a fee) you will not pay commissions on your preferred share purchases. This is because preferred share offerings commissions are paid by the offering company *not the buyer*!

So, when you buy a preferred share at $25 you pay $25 per share. (Some firms do charge a small ticket or transaction fee though.) The brokers commission is paid to them out of the offering. There should never be any commission to you. **This is a win for the broker and a win for the client**. Any business you give to the broker is a bonus to him or her. He or she earns by you buying preferred.

Additionally, the broker will want to call you each time an issue meets your criteria knowing you may have an interest.

They are your alert system to new issues on the way. Now you know all the new issues that your broker's firm has access too.

Lastly, it builds the broker's money under management which the broker and the firm like as well.

New Issue Alert Services

Because of the unique way preferred shares are funded, marketed and sold the biggest issue is knowing when they are going to begin trading or go public. There are a few ways to know when issues are coming out.

First your broker. A good broker will notify you when new issues of preferred become available. The problem I have encountered though is laziness. Initially the broker will call with *every* preferred and then, over time, forget to call or call only on occasion.

The second way is to look through the Edgar system for new issues. It's not easy but I know people who look daily at all new filings.

Lastly, there are spotting services who will notify you by email when most of the issues are coming out.

Because new preferred issues file and list at a moment's notice many can give you ample time to prepare to purchase new shares. Other times it's so quick that even the spotting services can get caught flat-footed. Overall, services that alert you to when issues are arriving are an important part of investing in preferred stocks as they provide a new flow of high dividend players and help you to replenish your account when others are called.

Typically, these services cost $30-$100 per month. Not a great expense when you think about the potential for profit.

Over the years I have had an email alert I send to friends who now follow preferred stock investing. The email list had grown to the point whereby it has become a pay-for service to monitor just about every new issue coming.

Newsletters and Other Free Resources

Nobody likes investing alone. The field for preferred shares is relatively small compared to the rest of the investment world. This small corner does have a few bloggers commenting on sites like *Seeking Alpha*. I'll mention a few and my thoughts.

Mark Grant is a blogger on *Seeking Alpha*. The managing director of *B. Riley*, a brokerage firm that does a lot of smaller edgier preferred stock offerings, he also has written a book. Mark is undoubtably one of the most knowledgeable preferred stock investors in the world. He has seen it all. His knowledge is wide about the economy and interest rates and is regularly quoted by the mainstream media when they need to get a handle on what's going on. In this book, I shared with you his mantra that 'risk is a monster.'

Mark is a 'big picture guy.' He is the type of guy that you as a preferred investor you should follow. If *he* gives a warning – **heed that warning**!

Lastly Mark in his blog doesn't usually talk about specific issues of preferred. Instead he merely comments on market and rate conditions and keeping to your goal of only buying quality issues. His blog is free here: https://seekingalpha.com/author/mark-j-grant#regular_articles

Seeking Alpha. Remember not everyone's interests are in your best interests. There are many bloggers who write for *Seeking Alpha* who either are not sufficiently knowledgeable on preferred shares or may *and I say **may** have an unsavory agenda. Either way, stick to the rules of investing and do not be swayed by a story of some fledgling preferred. If some story catches your eye, research its validity yourself and understand many preferred are full of risk. **A sucker's born every minute and we do not want you to be that sucker.**

Preferred Stock Channel. It's been said you get what you pay for and Preferred Stock Channel is free. The site is a decent resource to use and when asked I often tell folks to use it as a reference but know much on the site is not current. There is a lot of information there and it can quickly help you find an issue you might have an interest in. But, as mentioned, the only issue I have with the site is sometimes it's not accurate. Old issues that have been called might still appear as not called, while others not called might say called! Again, the site is free to use. They make money from advertising.

You can check out my website for yourself, it's called **preferredstockdatabase.com** and gives up-to-date information on all preferred shares. My aforementioned alert system notifies subscribers when a new preferred stock or preferred stock IPO goes public.

You can sign up here:
PREFERREDSTOCKALERT.COM

Vocabulary Toolkit

KEY TERMS

Adjustable-Rate Preferred Stock
Pays a dividend that is adjustable, usually quarterly, based on changes in the Treasury bill rate or other money market rates.

Call
The right to 'call back' or redeem a firm's outstanding preferred stock by paying the preferred stockholders the par value of the stock.

Callable
Preferred shares that may be redeemed early by the issuer, generally after five years from issuance date.

CD
Bank's certificate of deposit.

Compounding Frequency
Compounding frequency is the number of times per year the accumulated interest is paid out, or credited to an account, on a regular basis. The frequency could be yearly, half-yearly, quarterly or monthly.

Compound Interest
Compound interest is interest on interest. It is the result of reinvesting interest, rather than taking it out, so that interest in the next period is then earned on the principal sum plus previously accumulated interest. Compound interest may be contrasted with simple interest, where interest is not added to the principal, so there is no compounding.

Convertible

Preferred shares that have a conversion feature, allowing them to be converted into common stock of the issuing company. There are instances, however, when this feature is provided to the issuer of the security, such as a mandatory conversion at a future date.

Current yield

Calculated by dividing the annual coupon payment by the current market price of the stock.

Cumulative

Most preferred stock is cumulative; if dividends are passed (not paid for any reason), they accumulate and must be paid before common dividends. When a company fails to make a dividend or interest payment those payments accrue and must be paid in a future payment to a cumulative preferred shareholder before distributions can be made to any common shareholders.

Cumulative vs. Non-Cumulative

For cumulative preferred shares, if the issuer misses a dividend or interest payment, interest accrues to holders and must be paid in full before the issuer can resume preferred or common stock payments. Usually payments can be deferred for up to 60 months, during which the holder may still be responsible for paying taxes on accrued but unpaid interest or dividends. For non-cumulative preferred shares, when payments are missed, they do not accrue to holders and are unlikely to be paid in the future.

Dutch Auction Preferred Stock

A type of adjustable-rate preferred stock whose dividend is determined every seven weeks in a 'dutch' auction process by corporate bidders. Shares are bought and sold at face values ranging from $100,000 to $500,000 per share.

DRD

Dividends-received deduction. Indicates that the security is eligible for the dividends-received deduction to U.S. corporations. This allows 70% of the dividends received from the preferred stock to be excluded from the corporation's taxes. This tax benefit does not have an expiration date.

Extraordinary Call

Investments with extraordinary call provisions give the issuer the right to redeem a security before the maturity date due to unforeseen or unusual circumstances. Reasons an issuer might use an extraordinary call provision include asset sales, covenant violations and tax law changes. The terms of the redemption are stipulated in the securities prospectus. Securities with extraordinary call provisions require extra review by investors. If you buy a security with an extraordinary call provision at a price above par value, and the security is called, you would just receive par value, and give up all the premium you paid for the security.

Fixed-To-Float Preferred

Fixed-to-float preferred stock carry a fixed dividend rate at issuance for a period usually 3, 5 or 10 years. After it becomes callable by the issuer with 30-days' notice. If the issuer doesn't call the preferred stock the issues dividend rate will begin to float and reset for as long as the issue remains outstanding as cited by prospectus. Typically, the new dividend rate begins floating, based on Three-Month LIBOR (The London Inter Bank Offered Rate) plus a percentage listed in the prospectus.

IPO

Initial public offering.

LIBOR

Libor or The London Interbank Offered Rate, is the leading benchmark interest rate index used to make adjustments to variable-rate loans and credit cards. LIBOR is used by world banks when charging each other for short-term loans as well as derivatives and other financial products. When a loan rate moves up or down, a changing LIBOR rate is partially responsible.

LIBOR is based on five currencies:

- U.S. dollar (USD)
- Euro (EUR)
- Pound sterling (GBP)
- Japanese yen (JPY)
- Swiss franc (CHF)

LIBOR serves maturities that range from overnight to one year. The most commonly quoted rate is the three-month U.S. dollar rate. The Wall Street Journal publishes LIBOR rates daily.

NYSE

New York Stock Exchange.

Next Call Date
The next date that the issuer has the option to redeem the security. Once a preferred security first call date has passed, the issuer can redeem the security anytime within 30 days, notice.

Non-Cumulative Preferred Stock
A preferred stock issue in which unpaid dividends do not accrue. Such issues contrast with cumulative preferred issues, where unpaid dividends accumulate and must be paid before any dividends are paid on common shares. Most preferred issues are cumulative. Noncumulative preferred omitted dividends, generally, are not paid and are gone forever.

OTC
Over-the-Counter (prior to being traded on the exchange.)

Par Value
Face value of a preferred stock that is the price that will be paid at maturity. Preferred stock dividends normally are stated as a percentage of the assigned par value.

Passed Dividend
Dividends customarily paid on common shares that the board of directors fails to declare, usually because of financial strife at the company; sometimes called an 'omitted dividend'. On cumulative preferred stock, a passed dividend on shares accrues until paid.

Preferred Stock
Class of capital stock that pays dividends at a specified rate that has preference over common stock in the payment of dividends and liquidation of assets. It usually pays dividends at a fixed rate, but there is also adjustable rate preferred. For example, 6% preferred stock means that the dividend equals 6% of the total par value of the outstanding shares. Except in unusual instances, no voting rights exist. Preferred stock is sometimes called preference stock. Banks and bank holding companies have issued several classes of preferred stock, including perpetual preferred stock, which has no stated maturity date and is not redeemable by the holder; and limited life preferred stock, or preferred stock with a stated maturity of at least 25 years.

Under the risk-based capital guidelines adopted by U.S. banking regulatory agencies for bank holding companies and state-chartered banks that are members of the Federal Reserve System, nonvoting preferred stock can be counted as part of a bank's core capital or Tier 1 capital. (Tier 1 capital must equal 4% of a bank's total assets.) Preferred stock eligible for inclusion as Tier 1 capital can be noncumulative preferred stock, equal to 25% of common stock but not auction rate preferred stock, such as money market preferred stock.

QDI - Qualified Dividend Income.
Indicates that the security pays dividend income that qualifies for the reduced dividend tax rates to individuals.

Ratings Composite
The average of the preferred securities existing credit ratings by Moody's, S&P, Fitch and DBRS. NR = not rated.

Redemption
The right to call or redeem a firm's outstanding preferred stock by paying the preferred stockholders the par value of the stock.

SEC
Securities Exchange Commission.

Stated Call
A security with a stated call can be redeemed prior to maturity at the issuer's discretion on specified dates at specified prices.

Strip Price
The strip price removes the accrued dividend from a preferred exchange-traded price to get a better reflection of the underlying value of the security.

Symbol / CUSIP
The preferred securities trading symbol if applicable. Otherwise, CUSIP is displayed.

Tier 1 Capital
Tier 1 capital is the core measure of a bank's financial strength from a regulators point of view. It is composed of core capital, consisting of common stock, disclosed reserves (retained earnings) and non-redeemable non-cumulative preferred stock. The theoretical reason for holding capital is that it should provide protection against unexpected losses.

Yield to Call (YTC).
The realized yield if a security is held until the first call date, assuming all dividends are reinvested at the call rate and taking into account any income

and capital gains or losses.

Yield to Maturity (YTM)

The yield of the preferred if held to final maturity and dividends are reinvested at the yield-to-maturity rate, taking into account the income earned and any capital gain or loss that will be made. For example, an investor has to consider redemption at a lower price if a preferred is bought at a premium and held to maturity, as the holder will only receive the par at maturity.

Yield to Worst (YTW).

The lower of either the yield to maturity or the yield to call. Generally, if the preferred share is trading at a premium to par, the yield to call will be lower and the preferred is more likely to be called. However, if it is trading at or below par, the yield to maturity will be lower and it is more likely not to be called.

ABOUT THE AUTHOR

Writer, investor and investment banker, Herbert Tabin
is the author of five books about money, technology and
politics. He has been featured on the cover of
Entrepreneur Magazine and was nominated for
Ernst and Young's 'Entrepreneur of the Year',
receiving 'The Award for Business Leadership'.
Now a full-time writer, Mr. Tabin and his wife call
South Florida home.
You can visit him at
thebillionairessecret.com or
preferredstockdatabase.com

www.ingramcontent.com/pod-product-compliance
Lightning Source LLC
Chambersburg PA
CBHW021928190326
41519CB00009B/952